English Idioms
Exercises on Idioms

Jennifer Seidl

A second edition of Idioms in Practice

Oxford University Press

Oxford University Press,
Walton Street, Oxford OX2 6DP

Oxford New York Toronto
Delhi Bombay Calcutta Madras Karachi
Petaling Jaya Singapore Hong Kong Tokyo
Nairobi Dar es Salaam · Cape Town
Melbourne Auckland

and associated companies in
Berlin Ibadan

Oxford and *Oxford English* are
trade marks of Oxford University Press.

ISBN 0 19 432772 8

First edition 1982 (reprinted 4 times)
Second edition 1989
Fourth impression 1991

Illustrations by Diana Gold

Set by Pentacor Ltd, High Wycombe
Printed in Hong Kong

Contents

List of exercises

Introduction

About this book

English Idioms: Exercises on Idioms is one of two practice books which accompany the reference volume *English Idioms* (fifth edition, 1988) by Seidl and McMordie. It is a revised, up-dated edition of *Idioms in Practice* (1982).

Exercises on Idioms has been written for adolescent and adult learners who wish to widen their knowledge of, and improve their ability to use, idiomatic English. It is suitable for all learners from an intermediate level upwards, either as a first exercise book on idioms or as a revision and practice book.

Contents

The book contains 125 exercises on all the types of idioms presented in *English Idioms*. Over 800 of the most common idioms are practised and tested by means of a variety of exercise types.

Organization

The order of the exercises follows the arrangement of the reference volume *English Idioms*, where all the idioms practised are explained and illustrated with examples. Page references to *English Idioms* are given at the beginning of each exercise. Exercises are also clearly labelled to show the structures or items being practised.

How to use the book

Exercises on Idioms can be used as a classroom or self-study companion to *English Idioms*. It can also be used on its own by students wishing to revise their knowledge of idioms. The answer key provides an instant check.

In the classroom the book is an ideal supplement to a course book or grammar. Exercises can be worked through in the order in which they appear, or individual verbs, structures or key words can be chosen for practice according to need and interest.

Key words with idiomatic uses

Adjectives and adverbs

1 bad (EI 14-15)

Complete the sentences with the correct idiom in the correct form.

a bad lot
be in someone's bad books
go from bad to worse
a bad patch
give something up as a bad job
make the best of a bad job

▷ I started a crossword puzzle last night, but it was too difficult for me, so I soon _____ .
gave it up as a bad job

1 Liz asked me to wash the dishes but I forgot, so I'm afraid I _____ .
2 Don't trust Barry Parker. He's always in trouble with the police. In my opinion he's _____ .
3 There isn't much chance of getting a job in this part of the country. The unemployment figures have risen again here. The situation _____ .
4 The British economy has certainly been going through _____ but there are definite signs of improvement now.
5 John couldn't persuade the bank to lend him as much as he wanted, so he's going to _____ and sell his car to pay for the repairs to the roof.

2 big (EI 15-16)

Substitute for the phrase in *italics* an idiom from the list with the same meaning.

a big hit
make it big
a big noise
a big mouth
give someone a big hand
in a big way

▷ Alex says he could afford a new Mercedes every year, but I don't believe him. He's just *a boastful talker*.
a big mouth

1 The new teacher is *very popular* with the children.
2 Harry's opening up a chain of boutiques on the south coast. He's going into business *on a large scale*.
3 Jefferson's *an influential person* from the Ministry of Defence. Didn't you know?
4 Pamela played beautifully in the school concert. The audience *applauded enthusiastically*.

5 Peter was hoping to *be very successful* in the fashion world, but he couldn't get his designs manufactured.

3 dead (EI 16-17)

Complete the sentences with the correct idiom in the correct form.
be dead against something
make a dead set at someone
a dead loss
a dead end
cut someone dead
dead right

▷ 'Have you been able to persuade your father to buy a computer?' 'No, he ____ the idea.'
is dead against

1 I had difficulty in finding the way. I took a wrong turning and it was ____ .
2 Why won't Mary speak to me? She simply ____ in the bank yesterday.
3 You warned me that I'd be sorry if I bought an old car, and you were ____ . I've paid a fortune in repairs.
4 Mark can play the violin beautifully but he's ____ at anything practical.
5 David behaved badly during the meeting. He ____ Andrew without any provocation whatsoever.

4 flat (EI 17-18)

Substitute for the phrase in *italics* an idiom from the list with the same meaning.
go flat out
tell someone flat
and that's flat
fall flat
knock someone flat
in two minutes flat

▷ There was very little traffic on the motorway, so I *drove as fast as I could* all the way and got here early.
went flat out

1 I won't have your Uncle Fred to stay. Don't ask me again. I've said no *and it's my final word*.
2 Jeff wanted to borrow some more money, but I *told him quite definitely* that I won't give him any.
3 The Jacksons were going to buy a bigger house, but their plans *didn't materialize* because Mr Jackson lost his job.
4 The tragic news of Peter's accident *stunned me*.
5 I've never seen a child eat so quickly. She finished a plate of chicken and chips *in no more than two minutes*!

5 good (EI 18-20)

What's missing? Complete the sentences using an idiom from the list.

do you a good turn
be as good as gold
do you good
be for good
have a good time

1 Come on, take it! It will _____ .

2 Now remember, I want you to _____ .

3 _____ and send me a postcard.

4 I wonder if it will _____ this time.

5 Thanks a lot. Let me know if I can ever _____ .

6 hard (EI 20-1)

Complete the sentences by choosing the correct idiom.

▶ The management is determined to _____ with the union and refuse all their demands.
play hard to get   have a hard time   take a hard line
take a hard line

1 Motorists have been _____ by the sudden rise in the price of petrol.
hard pressed   hard to please   hard hit   hard up

2 Can you give me _____ for the use of the present perfect?
a hard nut to crack   a hard line   a hard and fast rule

3 This shop won't accept credit cards or cheques, only _____ .
the hard stuff   hard cash

4 We asked Joanna Walker to be our guest speaker, but she hasn't definitely accepted yet. She's obviously _____ .
driving a hard bargain   taking a hard line   playing hard to get

5 I need a new coat but I can't afford one. I'm a bit _____ at the moment.
hard hit   hard pressed   hard up   hard to please

7 high (EI 21-2)

Substitute for the phrase in *italics* an idiom from the list with the same meaning.
high and low
high and dry
get on one's high horse
be in high spirits
be for the high jump
a high flyer

▶ Philip is aiming at getting a seat on the board of directors. I don't think he has the necessary experience, but he always was *a very ambitious person*.
a high flyer

1 I think Rachel must have had some good news. She has *been in a very cheerful mood* all day.

2 I bought some new gloves last week and now I can't find them. I've looked *everywhere possible* for them.

3 David could be quite a nice person to work with, if only he didn't *behave in an arrogant manner* every time you asked him his opinion.

4 If the teacher finds out that you cheated in the maths test you'll *be due for severe punishment*.

5 I missed both the last bus and the last train. If I hadn't found a taxi I would have been left *isolated*.

8 hot (EI 22)

Which is correct?

1 An area of political unrest or danger is called _____ .
   a hot seat   a hot line   a hot spot
2 If you 'hot on something' you _____ .
   like it very much   are very knowledgeable about it   want to have it very much
3 If you 'blow hot and cold' you _____ .
   are feeling ill   are undecided   are very angry
4 If you 'make it hot for someone' you _____ .
   warm up the room for him   make things difficult for him   make him angry
5 Someone who is irritated or annoyed is said to be _____ .
   in hot water   piping hot   hot under the collar

9 long (EI 23)

Explain the meaning of the idioms in *italics*.

▷ 'Did you enjoy the film on Channel 4 last night?' 'It wasn't bad, but the story was too *long drawn out* in my opinion.'
slow-moving, lengthy

1 Jan gave me three good reasons why she can't come to Rome with me, but *the long and the short of it* is that she doesn't want to.
2 I know it's *a long shot*, but couldn't the missing report have been sent to head office by mistake?
3 Penny knows just what she wants in life. She's a girl who will *go a long way*.
4 James is working hard learning Russian. He's convinced that it will be worth it *in the long term*.
5 'Either we pay a lot of money for repairs and rust removal, or we sell the car and buy a smaller second-hand one.' 'If you ask me, it's *as broad as it's long*.'

10 old (EI 23-4)

Which is correct?

1 A narrow-minded person with old-fashioned ideas can be called _____ .
an old hand   the old man   an old fogey

2 A male person of authority can be called _____ .
the old school   the old man   a chip off the old block

3 A person with a lot of experience, skill or practice can be called _____ .
an old hand   the old school   an old flame

4 A son/daughter very like his/her father in character is called _____ .
old hat   a chip off the old block   an old fogey

5 A person one was attracted to in the past is called _____ .
an old hand   an old flame   the old school

11 short (EI 24-5)

Complete the sentences with the correct idiom in the correct form.

I'm surprised to see that you _____ the report. I thought it would take you much longer.
fall short of   go short of   make short work of
made short work of

1 I'm afraid I've _____ of coffee. Would you like tea instead?
be taken short   go short   run short

2 I was christened Elizabeth, but most people call me Beth _____ .
in short   at short notice   for short

3 We didn't enjoy the film very much. It _____ our expectations, after all the talk about it and the good write-up in the press.
fall short of   run short of   be short with

4 Her letter is _____ . It just says that she won't be coming after all.
in short supply   short and to the point   at short notice

5 What he's suggesting is _____ fraud. I want nothing to do with it.
little short of   short of   a short cut

12 **thick, thin** (EI 25-6)

Which idiom with *thick* or *thin* describes the picture?

1   He's *having a thin time.*
    thin on top.
    got a thick skin.

2   He's *laying it on thick.*
    in the thick of it.
    skating on thin ice.

3   They're *in the thick of it.*
    laying it on thick.
    skating on thin ice.

4   He's *vanished into thin air.*
    as thin as a rake.
    the thin end of the wedge.

5   They're *thick on the ground.*
    as thick as two short planks.
    as thick as thieves.

Nouns

13 end (EI 26-7)

Substitute for the phrase in *italics* an idiom from the list with the same meaning.
at the end of the day
go off at the deep end
to no end
make ends meet
get hold of the wrong end of the stick
in the end

▷ With higher taxes, lower profit margins and reduced export opportunities small businesses can hardly *manage with the money they earn*.
make ends meet

1 I tried to explain to Pete how the accident happened, but when he saw the damage to his car he *became angry* and started shouting at me.
2 Jane asked Bill if he had time to drive her home, but he *misunderstood her intention* and asked her over to his flat.
3 We had to fight with the finance department to persuade them not to cut our production budget, but *finally* we won.
4 We've tried several times to persuade Dad to come and live with us, but it's all *in vain*. He wants to stay in his own house.
5 I admit that Babs is sometimes arrogant, but *when all has been considered*, she's the best player in the team and she deserves to be captain.

14 line (EI 27-9)

Substitute for the phrase in *italics* an idiom from the list with the same meaning.
somewhere along the line
drop someone a line
fall into line with something
take the line of least resistance
get a line on someone
right down the line

▷ Don't forget to *write to us* as soon as you arrive.
drop us a line

1 'Has Max decided how to get out of his dilemma?' 'No, but if I know Max, he'll *find the easiest way of doing it*.'
2 'The drop in profits proves that we adopted the wrong advertising policy.' 'Yes, it's clear that we made the wrong decisions *at every stage*.'
3 These calculations aren't correct. *At some stage* I must have made a mistake.
4 You can't expect Gina to *agree to accept* our proposal if you don't give her all the details.
5 If you want to *find out information about* Walker for your newspaper article, ask Carol Richards. She used to work with him.

15 matter (EI 29)

Complete the sentences by choosing the correct idiom.

no laughing matter
no matter who
a matter of opinion
a matter of time
a matter of life and death
a matter of concern

▷ John's my nephew and his future is naturally ＿＿＿ to me.
a matter of concern

1 Harry is taking the exam too seriously. From what he says, you would think passing it is ＿＿＿ .
2 If there are any phone calls, ＿＿＿ it is, tell them I'm not here.
3 Whether state education or private education is best for a child is ＿＿＿ .
4 Gerald says it's ＿＿＿ being in hospital with a broken leg.
5 Jenny hasn't realized her mistake yet, but she will. It's just ＿＿＿ .

16 mind (EI 29-31)

Explain the meaning of the idioms in *italics*.

▷ Helen said she'd lend me a book on Chinese music, but she hasn't brought it with her. *It must have slipped her mind.*
She must have forgotten about it.

1 *I've a good mind* to take this pullover back to the shop and complain. When I washed it the colour came out.
2 I can't *make up my mind* whether to accept the job in New Zealand or go to Brussels where I'll earn more money.
3 A family in Madrid is advertising for an exchange student for the summer. *I've half a mind* to write to them.
4 Maureen seems very preoccupied this morning. She must *have a lot on her mind*.
5 If I were you, I wouldn't let your father-in-law interfere so much. It's time you *spoke your mind* and told him that you can bring the children up yourself.

17 point (EI 31-2)

Complete the sentences by choosing the correct idiom.

▷ In my opinion, Brian's much too young to get married. But what I think is ＿＿＿ . He never listens to what I say.
the sticking point   a sore point   beside the point
beside the point

1   I know you never lend things, but ____ and let me borrow
your guitar. I promise I'll take good care of it.
miss the point   stretch a point   come to the point

2   Don't waste so much time! ____ and let's get on with the rest
of the business.
see the point   wander off the point   get to the point

3   I'm afraid I can't ____ writing a six-page letter when you
could settle the matter in two minutes on the telephone.
make a point of   be on the point of   see the point of

4   I suppose I could write a long letter of complaint to the
manufacturers, but then, ____ . They won't give me a new
washing machine.
what's more to the point   that's the whole point   what's the point?

5   John probably told you that he had no trouble getting into
university, but ____ he had four refusals before he finally got a
place.
not to put too fine a point on it   in point of fact   point taken

18   thing   (EI 33)

Complete the sentences by
choosing the correct idiom.
not quite the thing
just one of those things
just the thing
a thing of the past
a near thing
sure thing!

▷ Fiona never mentions her ex-husband. Her marriage
is ____ to her.
a thing of the past

1   'Did Tony pass the exam?' 'Yes, but only just. His teacher told
him that it was ____ .'

2   'Could you post these letters for me?' '____ . I'm just on my
way to the post office.'

3   You can't possibly invite guests to the reception and expect them
to pay for food and drinks themselves. It's ____ .

4   'Would this screwdriver be of help?' 'Oh, it would be ____ .'

5   Barbara lost her purse and she's very upset about it. It's
unfortunate, but ____ .

19 way (EI 33-5)

Substitute for the phrase in *italics* an idiom from the list with the same meaning.

go out of one's way
go one's own way
mend one's ways
have it both ways
have one's own way
have a way with something

▶ Don and Sally *did everything possible* to help me when my wife was in hospital.
went out of their way

1 Mary's got a very strong personality. She always manages to *get what she wants*.
2 You want plenty of free time and a successful career, but you can't *have two opposing things*. Either get a decent job or be a drop-out.
3 Steve does nothing but enjoy himself at university. If he doesn't *improve his attitude* and do some work, he'll fail the final exams.
4 All dogs and horses seem to love Jane. She obviously *has a talent for dealing with* animals.
5 Bill won't listen to anyone's advice on careers. He's determined to *do things independently*, even if he makes mistakes.

20 word (EI 35-6)

Complete the sentences with the correct idiom in the correct form.

▶ Lucy said that she'd baby-sit for us on Saturday evening, so as long as she ____ , we'll be able to go to the concert after all.
keep one's word   have the last word   mince one's words
keeps her word

1 Barry swears that he isn't responsible for the damage and since I can't prove it, I'll have to ____ .
have the last word   go back on one's word   take someone's word for it
2 It's no use translating idioms ____ . They hardly ever make sense.
in a word   word perfect   word for word   by word of mouth
3 Helen's been neglecting her homework lately. I'll ____ with her parents about it.
have words   have the last word   have a word
4 It's no use trying to argue with Father. He's always convinced that he's right and he always ____ .
give someone one's word   mince one's words   have the last word
5 This is Emma's birthday present, but remember, ____ or you'll spoil the surprise.
that's not the word for it   from the word go   mum's the word

21 world (EI 37)

Explain the meaning of the idioms in *italics*.

▷ Mick's father has offered to buy him a new guitar, but he won't part with his old one, *not for the world.*
under no circumstances

1 Sheila says she doesn't want to have a career and *get on in the world.* She's much happier helping Jim at the garage.
2 Charles has got to know a young artist. He says her paintings are really *out of this world.*
3 Mrs Briggs used to run her own business, but now she's working as a shop assistant. Why has she suddenly *come down in the world?*
4 Harry's obviously feeling *on top of the world* this morning. He's laughing and joking with everyone.
5 No one would think that Brian and Gordon are brothers. They're *worlds apart.*

Miscellaneous

22 all (EI 37-41)

Which is correct?

1 When a person says he's 'all in' it means ⎯⎯.
he has arrived   he is very tired   he has finished packing
2 When a person is described as being 'all there' it means ⎯⎯.
he has arrived   he has got everything   he is clever and alert
3 When something is described as being 'all the rage' it ⎯⎯.
is very popular   makes people angry   is on fire
4 When someone says 'for all I care' it indicates that he ⎯⎯.
cares a lot   doesn't care at all
5 If something costs 'all of £2000' it costs ⎯⎯.
less than £2000   exactly £2000   at least £2000

23 how (EI 41)

Complete the sentences by choosing the correct idiom.
how on earth?
any old how
how come?
and how!
how's it going?
how about?

▶ I'm afraid Johnny doesn't take much care over his homework. He usually does it _____ .
any old how

1 If Monday doesn't suit you, _____ Friday?
2 'I heard that you really enjoyed the musical *Cats*.' 'Oh yes, we did, _____ .'
3 _____ Sarah hasn't invited you to her party? I thought you were good friends.
4 _____ do you expect me to get through all this work by Friday?
5 Fred! Nice to see you! _____ .

24 *it* as subject (EI 42-3)

Explain the meaning of the idioms in *italics*.

▶ *It's a bit off*, asking me to baby-sit four times in one week without any payment.
it isn't fair

1 I dropped this glass vase on the kitchen floor. *It's a wonder* that it didn't break.
2 Bill boiled his nylon shirts and they were all ruined. *It beats me* how anyone could be so stupid.
3 'Both teams are playing well. Who do you think will win?' 'Well, at the moment *it's anybody's guess*.'
4 'Shall I buy French wine or Italian?' '*It makes no odds*. I can't tell the difference.'
5 'Julia left her suitcase unattended at Euston Station and it got stolen.' '*It serves her right*. She's always careless with her things.'

25 *it* as object (EI 43-9)

What's missing? Complete the sentences using an idiom from the list in the correct form.

jump to it!
blast it!
out with it
step on it
take it or leave it
sleep on it
be at it
catch it
take it easy
hold it!

1 We'll have to _____ if we want to be at the station on time.

2 I've _____ since six o'clock this morning. I need a rest.

3 He'll _____ when his mother sees what he's done.

4 I told you to clean up your room an hour ago. Now come on! _____ .

5 If you _____ for a few weeks, you'll soon be fit again.

6 That's fine. Now _____ .

7 Three hundred pounds and not a penny more. _____ .

8 _____ . What a mess!

9 Come on, _____ . Tell me what really happened at school.

10 I don't need your decision now. Why not _____ and let me know tomorrow.

26 that (EI 49-51)

Complete the sentences by choosing the correct idiom.
come to that
that's for sure
that does it!
that will do
that's torn it!
that's the ticket!

▷ That's the third time that the baker has given me stale bread. I shall never buy bread there again, _____ !
that's for sure

1 'If that big boy hits me, I shall hit him back.' '_____, son!'
2 Tony looks rather pale today. _____, he hasn't looked well for quite some time now.
3 _____, children. There's no need to be rude.
4 _____. That dark-haired shop assistant was rude to me again. I shall complain to the manageress now.
5 Oh, no! _____. I pressed the switch too early and now the machine's got stuck.

27 there (EI 51-3)

Explain the meaning of the idioms in *italics*.

▷ Someone told me that Mary's going into business with Pam. But I'm sure *there's nothing in it*. Mary would have told me.
it isn't true

1 *There's nothing to it*. Watch carefully and I'll show you.
2 I told Chris that I was short of money, and he lent me some *there and then*.
3 *There's nothing else for it*. We can't afford to run the car now, so we'll have to sell it.

4   'Is Brenda's new telephone number six double eight double four or six double four double eight?' 'Ah, *you've got me there*, I'm afraid.'
5   *There's no knowing what* he'll do if he finds out that you lied.

28 too (EI 53-4)

Complete the sentences by choosing the correct idiom.
too good to be true
too funny for words
too much of a good thing
too big for one's boots
too true!
too many cooks

▷ There he was up the ladder with the bucket of water over his head! It was _____ !
too funny for words

1   No more chocolate mousse for me, thank you. That would be _____ .
2   It's best to plan the staff Christmas party yourself. You know what they say about _____ .
3   I still can't believe that I've won the painting competition. It's _____ .
4   Jeremy used to be so nice, but since he was asked to give a television interview he's become _____ .
5   'The teaching profession used to be highly regarded, but it has lost a lot of its prestige.' '_____ . I even feel sorry for teachers these days.'

29 what (EI 55-7)

Substitute for the phrase in *italics* an idiom from the list with the same meaning.
what's the game?
has got what it takes
knows what's what
what is it to you?
and what not
and what's more

▷ Why do you want to know how much we borrowed from the bank? *Why does it interest you?*
What is it to you?

1   Louise would like to become a concert pianist, but she doesn't think that she *has got the necessary qualities.*
2   *What are you doing?* That money's mine. You can't simply put it in your pocket!
3   She's very good with figures – *in addition* she can use a computer.
4   The shop sells household goods – plastic bowls and buckets, brushes *and other things of a similar kind.*
5   If you're buying a second-hand car, ask Tom's advice first. He *is very knowledgeable.*

Idioms with nouns and adjectives

30 Noun phrases (EI 58-63)

Complete the sentences by choosing the correct idiom.

▷ They say that every family has _____, but if this affair becomes public it will certainly be the end of Smithson's political career.
an Aunt Sally   a blot on the landscape   a skeleton in the cupboard
a skeleton in the cupboard

1 Rachel is always day-dreaming, building _____. It's time she came down to earth and found herself a job.
pie in the sky   castles in the air   a tower of strength

2 I told you that after a few weeks Janet's enthusiasm for horse riding would vanish, and I was right. It was just _____.
a flash in the pan   a straw in the wind   a storm in a teacup

3 'Aunt Martha told us that she's going to mention John in her will.' 'Really? Well, that is _____, because John was never a favourite of hers.'
a blessing in disguise   a turn-up for the books   beginner's luck

4 'Joe was depending on a fifty thousand pound loan from the bank, but he has just heard that they will only lend him thirty thousand.' 'Oh dear. That puts _____, doesn't it?'
a spoke in his wheel   a cog in the wheel   a thorn in his side

5 Sarah works for a secretarial agency, but she makes _____ hairdressing in the evenings.
money for jam   a bit on the side   the luck of the draw

31 Noun phrases (EI 58-63)

Complete the conversation by choosing the correct idioms.

the tricks of the trade
a blessing in disguise
his own man
a cog in the machine
the gift of the gab
a pillar of society
another cup of tea
a mug's game
a piece of cake
a feather in his cap

'Have you heard about Sam? He says that losing his job was probably ___1___, because he was tired of being just one of a thousand wage-earners at the firm, just ___2___ . He thinks working for someone else is really ___3___ , when you can work for yourself. So he's going to open up his own business now, a computer shop.'

'Really! Well, it will be ___4___ if he makes a success of it. And I hope he will.'

'He's taking Jerry Dobson into partnership with him.'

'Jerry Dobson, eh? Now he's ___5___ . I don't like him at all.'

'Well, he may not be what one could call ___6___ , but he's the right sort of man to get a business going. He's a good talker.'

'Oh yes. Jerry's certainly got ___7___ . And it won't take him long to learn ___8___ .'

'I told Sam that having his own business certainly won't be ___9___ . It's hard work. But he's determined to be ___10___ at last, so I wish him good luck.'

32 Adjective + noun (EI 63-78)

Which idiom describes the picture?

1 *a tough customer*
   a flash Harry
   a queer customer

2 *a tight spot*
   a tight squeeze
   an unknown quantity

3   *a stuffed shirt*
    a flash Harry
    a clever dick

4   *a marked man*
    a doubting Thomas
    a square peg

5   *a close-run thing*
    a close thing
    a back-seat driver

33 Adjective + noun (EI 63-78)

Complete the conversation by choosing the correct idioms.

a soft spot
a live wire
plain sailing
a going concern
a blind date
a down payment
a flying visit
a confirmed bachelor
a snap decision
a bitter pill

'Hello, Richard! This is just ___1___ , I haven't got much time. I'm on my way to Pete Marsden's place. He's getting married tomorrow.'

'That is a surprise. Pete told me that he had become ___2___ after that sad affair with Judith, and that he would never marry.'

'Yes, that was ___3___ for him. But all that's forgotten now. He's marrying an Irish girl called Pat.'

'An Irish girl, eh? Pete always had ___4___ for Ireland. How did he meet her? Did his brother arrange ___5___ for him with yet another girl from his office?'

'No, nothing like that this time. They met on a skiing holiday, I think. I've never seen Pete so happy. She's ___6___ , I can tell you.'

'Well, I hope it wasn't ___7___ that he'll regret.'

'Oh, no. He's already made ___8___ on a new house and his boutique is ___9___ , so from now on everything should be ___10___ for him.'

34 Adjective + noun (EI 63-78)

Complete the sentences by choosing the correct idiom.

▷ 'If you see Ian, don't mention the cricket team. He expected to be made captain, but he wasn't.' 'Oh, I see. It's ____ with him, is it?'
a raw deal   foul play   a sore point
a sore point

1   Where's Jeff these days? The last time I heard from him he was in Cairo, and he was thinking about getting a job in Tokyo. He never stays in one place very long. He's what they call ____.
a fast worker   a rolling stone   a bright spark

2   'I didn't know that Jean was so friendly with her head of department.' 'Oh yes. Everybody knows – but nobody speaks about it. It's been ____ for months.'
a hole and corner business   an open secret   inside information

3   'Have the police found out who did the bank robbery?' 'No, not yet, but they're fairly sure it was ____, so they're questioning the staff very thoroughly.'
a marked man   foul play   an inside job

4   'Did Susan pass her exam?' 'Yes, but only just. It was ____. The pass mark was forty-five per cent and she got forty-six per cent.'
a narrow escape   a tight spot   a close thing

5   Come on, Brian, join in the fun! Don't be such ____!
a second fiddle   a cool customer   a wet blanket

Idiomatic pairs

35 Pairs of adjectives (EI 79-80)

Which is correct?

1 Arrangements that are decided or final are said to be _____.
   safe and sound   home and dry   cut and dried
2 A person in a cheerful mood may be described as being _____.
   hale and hearty   alive and kicking   bright and breezy
3 A place that looks clean and tidy is said to be _____.
   fair and square   spick and span   home and dry
4 A casual, relaxed person may be described as being _____.
   free and easy   meek and mild   slow but sure
5 A person who is no longer young but who is physically fit may be
   described as being _____.
   alive and kicking   safe and sound   hale and hearty

36 Pairs of nouns (EI 80-2)

Which idiom describes the
situation in the picture?

1 They're going at it _____.
   hook, line and sinker
   body and soul
   hammer and tongs

2 He's enjoying some _____.
   beer and skittles
   fun and games
   peace and quiet

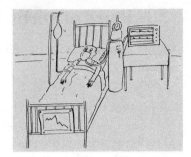

3   The house is going
to _____ .
bricks and mortar
rack and ruin
rough and tumble

4   He's critically ill. It's _____ .
life and limb
body and soul
touch and go

5   He's explaining some of
the _____ of football.
whys and wherefores
ifs and buts
ins and outs

37   Pairs of adverbs (EI 82-3)

Explain the meaning of the
idioms in *italics*.

▷ I've been looking for Cathy *here, there and everywhere*, but she
doesn't seem to be in the building at all.
in many different places

1   'Does Robin still visit you every week?' 'No, he lives in St. Albans
now, so he only comes *now and again*.'
2   Laura was very busy when I visited her. In fact, she *more or less*
asked me to leave. So I did.
3   There's been nothing good on television for weeks. Good
programmes are *few and far between*.
4   Personally I don't like the designs, but that's *neither here nor there*
because we're sure that they'll sell well.
5   'Does Sheila work full-time at the supermarket?' 'No, only *on
and off* when they need extra staff.'

38 Pairs of verbs (EI 83-4)

Complete the sentences with the correct idiom in the correct form.

grin and bear it
chop and change
toss and turn
pick and choose
give and take
wait and see

▷ Roy seems unable to decide on a suitable date. He's _____ all the time.
chopping and changing

1 If you book too late, the best hotels will be full up, so you won't be able to _____ . You'll have to take what's left.
2 I really can't tell you whether or not you have made the right decision. You'll simply have to _____ .
3 I had a dreadful toothache on Christmas Day. There was no dentist available so I had to _____ .
4 The patient _____ for at least an hour before he finally fell into a deep sleep.
5 If Pauline wants her marriage to work she'll have to learn how to _____ . Everyone has to make compromises.

39 Identical pairs (EI 85)

Substitute for the phrase in *italics* an idiom from the list with the same meaning.

blow by blow
on the up and up
all in all
bit by bit
again and again
by and by

▷ 'How's your father after his operation?' '*Improving* at last, I'm glad to say.'
on the up and up

1 I can't write the whole report today. I'll have to do it *in small stages*.
2 I've asked him *repeatedly* not to smoke in this room, but he doesn't seem to care.
3 I was unhappy in my new job at first, but *as time went by* I realized that it was the kind of challenge that I needed.
4 'Did you hear about John Smith's operation?' 'Yes, he gave me a *detailed* account – twice!'
5 We didn't win all the events, but *considering everything* our athletics team had a successful day.

Idioms with prepositions

40 above, across, after, against (EI 86)

Give a suitable short answer
with *Yes* or *No* and an idiom
from the list.
above par
above suspicion
across the board
above board
against the grain
after a fashion

▶ Do you think she could have stolen the money?
No, she's completely above suspicion.

1 Will Penny mind having to come into the office on Saturday?
2 Was the money transfer to the Swiss bank legal?
3 Has Robert cleaned his room at last?
4 Will the proposed wage increase benefit all the employees?
5 Is Jim feeling well after his long holiday?

41 at (EI 86-9)

Explain the meaning of the
idioms in *italics*.

▶ Matthew would leave his job and go abroad *at the drop of a hat*.
He's just waiting for a suitable opportunity.
willingly and immediately

1 I wish Joan and Mary wouldn't argue so much. They're always *at loggerheads* these days.
2 'When can you have the car repairs finished?' 'Well, by tomorrow evening, *at a push*.'
3 The teacher chose six pupils *at random* and asked them to help him in the school library.
4 Liz has lots of good contacts. When she started in business on her own she was offered help *at every turn*.
5 Surgeons sometimes have to operate for six hours or more *at a stretch*.

42 behind, below, by (EI 89)

Complete the sentences by choosing the correct idiom.
behind the scenes
behind closed doors
behind bars
by degrees
by leaps and bounds
below par

▶ A criminal record? Do you mean that he's been ＿＿ ?
behind bars

1 In film and TV studios, real drama often goes on ＿＿ .
2 I've been feeling ＿＿ for a week or so. I think it's influenza.
3 My French improved ＿＿ when I was working at our company's Paris branch.
4 Journalists were not admitted into the courtroom. The case was heard ＿＿ .
5 Japanese is a difficult language to learn. At first you'll only make progress ＿＿ .

43 for, from (EI 89-90)

Give a suitable short answer with *Yes* or *No* and an idiom from the list.
for keeps
for fun
from scratch
from cover to cover
for the asking
for kicks

▶ Have you given me this record? Is it mine now?
Yes, it's yours for keeps.

1 Did you read the book all the way through?
2 You mean, if Ben asks you for this valuable old clock he can have it?
3 Did those boys really break into the school just for the excitement?
4 Was Frank serious when he said that my car wouldn't pass its road test in a hundred years?
5 Did Jane have any previous knowledge of Russian when she started the course at university?

44 in (EI 90-3)

Complete the sentences by choosing the correct idiom.

1 'Marjorie's looking depressed.' 'Yes, she's been ＿＿ all day.'
   in the sticks   in a fog   in the dumps
2 'Are you quite sure it was Prince Charles you saw on the ski slope?' 'Yes. I tell you it was him ＿＿ .'
   in the open   in the flesh   in the limelight
3 Joe was telling some very funny stories last night. We were ＿＿ .
   in raptures   in full swing   in stitches

4 'Susan's been doing a lot of jogging recently.' 'Yes, she's really _____ now.'
in limbo   in step   in trim

5 Don't bother Pam just now. Something's gone wrong with the computer, so she's _____ because she can't get the data she needs.
in a stew   in a rut   in the swim

45 off *(EI 93-4)*

Which idiom with *off* describes the picture?

1 They are
off limits.
off the beaten track.
off the map.

2 He's buying a suit
off the rails.
off the peg.
off the cuff.

3 She's feeling
off colour.
off the mark.
off beam.

4 What she's saying is strictly
off the record.
off the air.
off limits.

5 He seems to be
off the rails.
off form.
off his own bat.

46 **on** (EI 94-7)

Complete the conversation by choosing the correct idioms.

on the dole
on the run
on the beat
on the rack
on the dot
on call
on the tiles
on the move
on the off-chance
on balance

'Hello, John!'

'Hello, Ken. I wasn't sure that you would be at home. I came ___1___ . How are you?'

' ___2___ , not too bad, but rather nervous at the moment. I'm waiting for the post to come. I'm expecting a letter with my examination results today.'

'Do you still want to study medicine?'

'Not really. Being a doctor has its disadvantages – you're ___3___ at weekends and sometimes at night.'

'Why not join the police force?'

'As a detective, yes, but for the first few years you're a constable ___4___ , or you're chasing escaped prisoners ___5___ . I wouldn't like that.'

'How about journalism?'

'No, you're ___6___ too much, never in one place for long. But I'll have to start applying for jobs soon, or I shall end up ___7___ , like thousands of others. Look, here's the postman. Nine o'clock ___8___ . And here's my letter!'

'Well, go on, open it! Don't leave me ___9___ !'

'It says I've passed with A grades in all subjects.'

'Wonderful! Congratulations!'

'Well, tonight we'll have a night ___10___ to celebrate.'

47 **out, over** (EI 97-8)

Which idiom with *out* or *over*
describes the picture?

1 He's
   out of condition.
   out of the running.
   out on a limb.

2 It looks
   out of bounds.
   out of place.
   out of sorts.

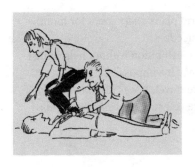

3 He's
   out of reach.
   out of condition.
   out for the count.

4 She's feeling
   out of the ordinary.
   out of character.
   out of sorts.

5 She's
   over the top.
   over the moon.
   over the hill.

48 round, to, under, up, within (EI 98-100)

Explain the meaning of the idioms in *italics*.

▶ 'What did he say?' 'I don't know. He just mumbled something *under his breath*.'
to himself, in a low whisper

1 Tim, please be quiet. You're driving me *round the bend* with your continual questions.
2 Patrick is very proud of his Irish heritage. He's an Irishman *to the core*.
3 How many students have registered for the course *to date*?
4 That's Anne *to a T*. That's precisely the kind of remark one would expect her to make.
5 I can take you there in my car, but you'll have to get back *under your own steam*.
6 Mr Harrison has a weak heart. He's been *under the doctor* for years.
7 The government kept the reform plans *under wraps* for months before they were finally announced.
8 If June thinks I can organize the exhibition without help in just one week, she must be *up the pole*. It's impossible.
9 Dennis loved the book on space travel. It was just *up his street*.
10 It's an expensive car to run. Are you sure it's *within our means*?

Phrasal verbs

49 be (EI 105-6)

Substitute for the phrase in *italics* an idiom from the list with the same meaning.
be into something
be down on someone
be in on something
be up against something
be in for something
be on to someone

▶ Apart from Jean and Bob, no one else *was informed about* the arrangements.
was in on

1 Paula *is likely to get* a nasty shock. Her car repairs will cost at least three hundred pounds.
2 Don't *be critical of* David all the time. He hasn't been trained for this type of work, so it isn't his fault if he's a bit slow.
3 The police seem to *be on the track of* the bank robbers. This newspaper report says they have concentrated their search on a particular area.
4 John has won all the local squash championships, but he'll *be confronted with* tough competition when he plays in the county championships.
5 I didn't know Sally *was very interested in* sky-diving. Isn't it dangerous?

50 break, bring (EI 107-9)

Which is correct?

1 What time do you expect the meeting to _____?
break down   break off   break up   break out
2 There was some fighting at the football match. When the police arrived they soon _____.
broke it off   broke in   broke with it   broke it up
3 The new secretary has been given the simple reports to type. The supervisor wants to _____ gently.
break through   break her in   break with her
4 There's talk of the Government _____ a new tax relief scheme for families with more than three children.
bringing off   bringing in   bringing up   bringing on

5 Robert had good reason to be pleased with himself.
He ＿＿＿ the deal with National Glass, although no one
expected him to.
brought up   brought off   brought round   brought in

6 I've got a headache. It must be the long spell of night driving
that ＿＿＿. The bright lights dazzle me.
brought it on   brought it out   brought it up

51 call, carry, catch (EI 110)

Complete the sentences with
the correct idiom in the correct
form.
call on someone
catch up
call for something
carry on
call for someone
catch on
call in

▶ I'll ＿＿＿ you on my way to work. Make sure you're ready!
call for

1 'The hospital's just rung up. Sheila's had twins!'
'Congratulations! This ＿＿＿ a celebration!'
2 Suddenly the chairman ＿＿＿ me to explain the results shown
on the computer printout.
3 Please ＿＿＿ with your work. Don't stop because of me.
4 The new record will appeal to older listeners, but I don't think it
will ＿＿＿ among younger pop fans.
5 I had to wait for over an hour in the doctor's waiting room, but at
least it gave me chance to ＿＿＿ with some reading.
6 Can we ＿＿＿ at the chemist's on the way to the bank? I need
some cough medicine.

52 come (EI 112-13)

Substitute for the phrase in
italics an idiom from the list with
the same meaning.
come along
come up
come to
come off
come across something
come in

▶ Dick loves making plans, but unfortunately they never seem to
succeed.
come off

1 We had a committee meeting last night. The subject of the new
table tennis equipment *was discussed*, and we decided to buy
three new tables.
2 How's the essay *progressing*? Have you finished it yet?
3 I *found* these old maps in an antique shop. They're probably
worth much more than I paid for them.
4 The first thing he did when he *regained consciousness* after the
accident was ask for a cigarette.
5 Short skirts are *becoming fashionable* again this summer.

53 cut, do (EI 113-15)

Explain the meaning of the idioms in *italics*.

▷ The van driving in front of us suddenly *cut off* into a side street and disappeared.
turned

1 I hate driving on motorways when lorries *cut in* so dangerously.
2 Jane *cut down on* bread and fatty foods and after only one week she had lost two pounds.
3 The news that the baby would have to go into hospital *cut her up* terribly.
4 *Do up* your shirt buttons. You look untidy.
5 Mr Jacobs left you the money in his will, so don't let anyone *do you out of it*. A few people may try.
6 I'm cold and tired. I *could do with* a hot drink.

54 get (EI 119-22)

Complete the sentences with the correct idiom in the correct form.

get over something
get down to something
get away with something
get by
get through
get on
get up to something
get at someone
get up
get out of something
get off

▷ Stop _____ me! I know it was my fault and I've said I'm sorry.
getting at

1 'Why are you so late?' 'I've been trying to ring Tokyo all morning and I only _____ five minutes ago.'
2 I'm very pleased to hear that your father has _____ his illness and is feeling well again.
3 'Shall I lend you some money?' 'No, thanks. Don't worry. I'll _____.'
4 I haven't had time to study the report in detail, but I hope to finally _____ it this afternoon.
5 Mike says that Billy _____ very well at his new school.
6 Children are full of mischief. When you leave them on their own, you can never be sure what they will _____ .
7 I know that Harry cheated at cards last night. If he tries to cheat again, I won't let him _____ .
8 I wasn't sure where to _____ , so I asked the bus driver.
9 Tim said he wasn't feeling well, but the teacher knew that he was only trying to _____ the history test.
10 I _____ at six o'clock this morning.

55 go (EI 123-5)

What's missing? Complete the sentences using an idiom from the list in the correct form.

go into something
go through with something
go for something
go off
go up
go on
go through something
go for someone

1 I can't eat this.
It's _____ .

2 How much did it _____ ?

3 Don't worry. I'm sure he won't _____ .

4 He looks fierce. I think he's going to _____ .

5 There's a lot of noise _____ up above.

6 Last week they were cheaper. Prices have _____ .

7 He's _____ the drawers.

8 The police will have to _____ the case very thoroughly.

56 hang, have (EI 125-6)

Explain the meaning of the idioms in *italics*.

▷ I'm sorry but I'll have to *hang up* now. I'll call you back later.
end the conversation

1 If you can *hang on* for a few minutes I'll fetch the file you need.
2 If I were you I would *hang on to* your dollars and exchange them when the rate goes up.
3 There's no point *hanging about* here. Roger won't be back for at least two hours.
4 Don't take what Ken says seriously. He's just *having you on*.
5 If you're not happy about the way Betty handled the situation, *have it out with her*.
6 We'd love to come with you, but we already *have something on* this evening. Another time perhaps.

57 hold (EI 127)

Complete the sentences with the correct idiom in the correct form.
hold something back
hold with something
hold something over
hold out for something
hold off
hold out

▷ John has all the facts I need, but he won't give them to me. He's deliberately _____ information _____ .
holding information back

1 Father doesn't _____ computerized records at all. He thinks traditional book-keeping is safer.
2 The car engine started making very strange noises, but thankfully it managed to _____ until I got home.
3 I don't think the union will accept a four per cent pay-rise. They'll _____ much more.
4 I strongly recommend that we _____ a discussion on item five until the next meeting, when we shall have the monthly sales figures.
5 Look at those black clouds. I hope the rain _____ until the game's over.

58 keep (EI 128-9)

Substitute for the phrase in *italics* an idiom from the list with the same meaning.

keep in
keep someone up
keep out of something
keep at something
keep in with someone
keep up with someone
keep on

▶ I want to *stay friendly with* Keith Barber. He's a good lawyer and I may need his advice soon.
keep in with

1 If you had *persevered with it*, you would have finished the book by now.
2 *Continue* with the medicine until your temperature is normal.
3 I'm sorry that I've *prevented you from going to bed*, but I thought you would want to hear the story in detail.
4 It's best to *stay indoors* when you've got a cold.
5 *Don't get involved in* that affair. It isn't your concern.
6 If you intend to *remain at the same level as* the rest of the class, you'll have to work harder.

59 look (EI 130-1)

Complete the sentences by adding the correct preposition or adverb to the verb *look*.

on
into
after
down
over
up
to
in
out

▶ Bill leaves the children with his sister when he goes out. He knows that they will be properly *looked* _____ .
after

1 These invoices must be *looked* _____ very thoroughly. There's a mistake somewhere.
2 Often when there's a traffic accident lots of people *look* _____ but no one offers to help.
3 Don is happy at work. He feels that his colleagues *look* _____ on him because he's the only one without a university degree.
4 *Look* me _____ when you're in Brazil next year.
5 There was a rumour about espionage activities, so counter-intelligence is *looking* _____ the matter very carefully.
6 Your temperature has gone down, Mrs Miller, but I want you to stay in bed and continue taking this medicine. I'll *look* _____ again tomorrow afternoon. Goodbye.
7 *Look* _____! If that box falls from the top of the cupboard when you open the door, it will hit you right on the head!
8 It's good to have someone to *look* _____ for help and advice in times of trouble.

60 make (EI 131-2)

Substitute for the phrase in *italics* an idiom from the list with the same meaning.

make out
make off
make something out
make someone out
make something up
make something over
make for something
make up for something
make off with something

▶ Janet's been behaving very strangely lately. I just can't *understand her.*
make her out

1 How did you *manage* at the interview? Do you think you'll get the job?
2 If I were you, I wouldn't believe all those stories. Old Bill loves *inventing things.*
3 What's wrong with Jerry? As soon as he saw me he *hurried away* in the opposite direction!
4 'Did you write down the number of the car?' 'No, unfortunately I couldn't *read it.*'
5 Henderson has *transferred* all his shares to his son, which virtually gives him a place on the board of directors.
6 The children were very hungry, so when we arrived home they *ran straight towards* the fridge and helped themselves to ice-cream.
7 The burglar was just about to *steal* the silver, when he was disturbed by the burglar alarm.
8 I'm so sorry that I forgot your birthday. How can I possibly *compensate for* it?

61 pass, play (EI 134-6)

Give a suitable short answer with *Yes* or *No* and an idiom from the list.

pass off
play up
pass for someone
pass out
play something down
pass on something
play along with someone
play up to someone
pass something on

▶ Don't you think John looks just like his brother?
Yes, he could pass for him easily.

1 Did Sheila faint?
2 Did the press make a big story of the affair?
3 Has the pain gone now?
4 Do you know the answer?
5 Isn't the machine working properly?
6 Do you think I should co-operate with Benson?
7 Did Margaret give Tim my message?
8 Have you seen how Bill flatters his boss when he wants something?

62 put (EI 137-8)

Substitute for the phrase in *italics* an idiom from the list with the same meaning.

put something off
put someone out
put up with something
put something up
put someone up
put someone off

▶ Can you concentrate, or is the noise of my typewriter *distracting you?*
putting you off

1 I've been thinking about *building* a greenhouse at the bottom of the garden, so that I can grow my own tomatoes.
2 We'd be very happy to *give you accommodation* if ever you're visiting Bath.
3 Please don't bother with lunch if it's too much trouble. I really don't want to *inconvenience you.*
4 I'm afraid I won't be able to meet you in town today. Could we *postpone it* until next week?
5 You'll have to *tolerate* the noise of the cement-mixer for a few more days.

63 run (EI 139-40)

Explain the meaning of the idioms in *italics.*

▶ If you happen to *run across* Pete, remind him that he owes me ten pounds, will you?
meet by chance

1 Tell me if you see a petrol station. I wouldn't like the petrol to *run out* on a country road.
2 Could you *run off* two hundred copies of this circular and distribute it to all departments immediately, please?
3 Of course James won't be lying in a hospital bed somewhere! You're letting your imagination *run away with you.*
4 Would you kindly *run through* my notes on the meeting and tell me if there are any mistakes?
5 We've *run up against* a few unexpected problems with the experiments. Gas seems to be escaping and we don't know why.

64 see (EI 141)

Give a suitable short answer
with *Yes* or *No* and an idiom
from the list.
see through someone
see to something
see someone off
see someone out
see something out
see something through

▷ Does Jim think that you believe his story?
Yes, but I can see through him.

1 Will you go with me to the station?
2 Did you watch the film to the end?
3 Could you show me the way to the main entrance?
4 Are you going to finish the project in spite of the additional costs?
5 Have you had the leak repaired in the kitchen?

65 set (EI 141-2)

Complete the sentences by
adding the correct preposition
or adverb to the verb *set*.
in
off
about
back
up
on

▷ Could you help me with this income tax form? I don't quite know how to *set* _____ it.
about

1 You had better prune your roses now, before the winter weather *sets* _____ .
2 We didn't expect you to arrive until after midnight. What time did you *set* _____ ?
3 After Mandy had finished her training and passed her exams, her father *set* her _____ in her own hairdressing salon.
4 We had a lovely evening out on Saturday, but it *set* me _____ over a hundred pounds!
5 The dog looked very fierce. In fact, we thought it was going to *set* _____ us at any minute.

66 sit, stand (EI 144-6)

Which is correct?

1 Sheila, would you kindly _____ Mary? She has a hospital appointment at ten o'clock tomorrow morning.
   stand up to   sit in on   stand in for   stand up for
2 Jim's very tall. He really _____ from the rest of his class.
   stands out   sits out   sits up
3 We _____ until midnight waiting for our teenage son to come home.
   sat in   stood by   sat up

4 Charles doesn't want to be re-elected chairman. He's going
   to _____.
   sit out   stand down   sit back   stand by

5 Polly's unfair. Instead of helping me with all the invitations, she
   just _____ and watched me write them all.
   sat out   stood out   sat back   stood down

67 take (EI 147-9)

Substitute for the phrase in
italics an idiom from the list with
the same meaning.

take up with someone
take someone on
take someone off
take someone in
take to someone
take after someone

▷ 'How do you like Vicky?' 'I'm not sure that I'll ever *form a liking
for her*. She seems rather arrogant and unfriendly.'
take to her

1 Bill's very popular with his workmates. One of the reasons is that
   he's very good at *imitating* all the directors.
2 Don't let yourself be *tricked* by people who try to sell things at the
   door.
3 The factory isn't *employing* any new workers until export orders
   improve.
4 What a bad temper that child has! Which of his parents does he
   resemble?
5 When Roger was in Cannes, he *became friends with* a rich French
   family who have a villa there.

68 turn (EI 151-2)

Complete the sentences with
the correct idiom in the correct
form.

turn out
turn up
turn something down
turn someone away
turn someone off something
turn someone over

▷ I used to love mathematics at school until we got a teacher who
was so boring that he _____ it completely.
turned me off

1 The chairman is very angry if committee members _____ late
   for meetings.
2 'How did your steak and kidney pie _____?' 'Not very well,
   unfortunately. I forgot the salt.'
3 Jim caught a burglar red-handed in his flat. The poor chap was
   more frightened than Jim was. He sobbed and pleaded with Jim
   not to _____ to the police.
4 Ruth wanted to be transferred to another department, but her
   application was _____ because her own department is
   understaffed.

5 There were still at least twenty people in the queue, but we had to _____ because all the tickets had been sold.

69 Nominalized forms (EI 104-54)

Which word describes the picture? Make short sentences using the correct word from the list.

a breakdown
a blow-up
a fall-off
a lie-in
a write-off
a cut-back
a tip-off
a hold-up
a check-out
a work-out
a check-up

▶ **Hands up! This is a hold-up!**

1

2

3

4

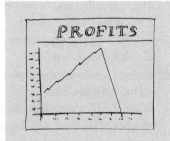

5

6

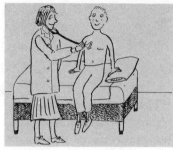

7   8

9   10

70 Nominalized forms (EI 104-54)

Explain the meaning of the words in *italics*.

▷ There's been some trouble between the union and the management. Tomorrow the workers are going to organize a *walk-out*.
sudden strike

1 Make sure that you count the money correctly this time. We don't want another *slip-up*.
2 Bob Elton was given a tremendous *write-up* when his latest album was released.
3 There's a *hold-up* on the motorway. A load of bricks has fallen off the back of a lorry.
4 When the fees were increased, there was a sudden *drop-off* in the number of students registering for the course.
5 Read this *hand-out* and be sure to come to the meeting tomorrow evening.

Verbal idioms

71 break, bring (EI 156)

Complete the sentences with the correct idiom in the correct form.

break the ice
break the bank
break the news
bring home the bacon
break fresh ground
bring something to light
bring someone to book
bring home to someone
break even

▶ Old Mr Johnson's dog has been knocked down by a lorry but he doesn't know about it yet. His neighbour's going to _____ to him.
break the news

1 'How was Sarah's party?' 'Oh, it was boring, until Mark managed to _____ by talking about a film that everyone had seen.'

2 That's the last time that I shall go to a casino. I didn't expect to _____, but I did expect to win a pound or two.

3 Professor Hart is a prominent biochemist. He's working on a project that is expected to _____ in genetics.

4 I wish Julia would do her work more carefully. This invoice is wrong again. I'll have to _____.

5 Joseph has been out of work for months. It's his wife who _____.

6 The police say that some new facts have been _____ in the Lord Beacon affair. On the night of the murder he made a strange phone call to Athens.

7 'Is Jane's new fashion boutique doing well?' 'Well, so far she has spent more money than she has earned, but she hopes to _____ by the end of next year.'

8 John was very lazy in school, but a serious talk with the careers master really _____ the importance of passing his school-leaving examination.

72 come (EI 158)

Substitute for the phrase in *italics* an idiom from the list with the same meaning.

come down to earth
come in handy
come to grips with something
come off second best
come unstuck
come clean

▷ In Frank's situation, it's best to *admit the truth* and tell the police everything.
come clean

1 I knew these old boxes would *prove their use* sooner or later. I need them now.
2 Penny is still dreaming about becoming a famous actress. It's time she *returned to reality* and worked harder at her job in the bank.
3 Janice wanted to open up a language school near Brighton, but for some unknown reason her plans *didn't materialize*.
4 You will have to *get control of* your problem. Why not join a discussion group? It may help to talk to people with the same difficulties.
5 I can understand Jim's disappointment. After all, who likes to *lose a competition*? Nobody!

73 do (EI 159-60)

Explain the meaning of the idioms in *italics*.

▷ Come to Oxford for the weekend and we'll *do the sights* together.
visit all the things worth seeing

1 Picnics are good fun, aren't they? Who's going to *do the honours* and open the wine?
2 My typewriter was making strange noises, so I cleaned it and oiled it and that *did the trick*. Now it's working perfectly again.
3 'How's your cough?' 'Much better , thanks. The doctor gave me some pills, and they're *doing wonders*.'
4 Joe sold Mac his car, although he knew that the engine was in a bad state. Instead of warning Mac, he *did the dirty* on him and let him think that the car was in perfect condition.
5 The doctors *did their level best*, but they couldn't save the patient.

74 get (EI 161-4)

Substitute for the phrase in *italics* an idiom from the list with the same meaning.

get the message
get the sack
get there
get the wind up
get in on the ground floor
get down to brass tacks
get one's own back
get a move on
get someone wrong
get nowhere
get the picture clear

▷ Since Bob *was dismissed* from the furniture factory, he hasn't bothered to look for a new job.
got the sack

1 Come on, Jack! *Hurry up!* I can't wait here all day!
2 We haven't much time for our meeting today, so I suggest we *start discussing the essential details* immediately.
3 Let me explain why I can't accept your invitation. I don't want you to *misunderstand my reasons*.
4 Graham should make a lot of money with his latest investment. He was lucky enough to *be involved from the start*.
5 You needn't look at your watch again. I've *understood what you want me to do* and I'll go now.
6 We've been trying to find the mistake in the computer programme all morning, but I'm afraid we're *making no progress*.
7 'How's your new book coming along?' 'Oh, I'm *slowly completing the task*. Thanks for asking.'
8 Thomas said that he would go sky-diving with me this weekend. But I think he's *become afraid*. He says he's not feeling very well.
9 Ron played a mean trick on me. But don't worry, I'll *get my revenge*.
10 If I have *understood the situation correctly* Jenny, Ken and Carol will be coming on the eighteenth and Bob and Richard two days later. Is that right?

75 give (EI 164-5)

Explain the meaning of the idioms in *italics*.

▷ I found her manner so unreasonable that I simply had to *give vent to* my anger.
express freely

1 The police followed the suspect to the end of the motorway, but then he managed to *give them the slip* by turning sharply into a narrow lane and disappearing.
2 We wanted to give you the book as a complete surprise on your birthday, but I suppose Ben *gave the game away* when he asked you if you had read it.
3 I've just been to the dentist's. It was awful. He really *gave me hell*.

4 People say that old, dark house is haunted. It *gives me the creeps* just passing by it.
5 Brian thought he would beat Jill easily when they played chess the other evening. In fact, he did eventually, but Jill certainly *gave him a good run for his money*.

76 go (EI 165-6)

Substitute for the phrase in *italics* an idiom from the list with the same meaning.

go the whole hog
go down well
go spare
go downhill
go phut
go by the board

▷ Margaret was delighted that her new television play *was received favourably*. The reviews were excellent.
went down well

1 When your father sees what you've done to his car he'll *become excessively angry*.
2 When we moved into the new house we didn't intend to buy new furniture. But Elizabeth said we ought to *make a thorough job of it*, so we did – and now we're in debt.
3 'What's wrong with the toaster?' 'It just *stopped working*.'
4 The food at this restaurant has been *deteriorating in quality* for some time now. I don't think I'll come here again.
5 When Jim broke his ankle the arrangements for our skiing holiday *were abandoned*.

77 have (got) (EI 166-8)

Complete the sentences with the correct idiom in the correct form.

have a say
have a crack at something
not have got a clue
have got a nerve
have got first refusal
have one's wits about one

▷ I've never made a Christmas pudding myself before, but I'm going to _____ it this year.
have a crack at

1 If Jack decides to sell his Volvo, I _____ , so don't expect him to offer it to you.
2 My parents ought to _____ in the matter too, since it concerns them. So please ask them as well.
3 'Who was the man who wanted to speak to me?' 'I'm sorry but I _____ . He wouldn't give his name.'
4 Go to bed early so that you won't be tired tomorrow. You will have to _____ at the oral exam.
5 Just imagine! Jeremy has told his friends that they are all invited to our party. I don't even know them. He _____ !

78 keep (EI 169-70)

Complete the sentences with the correct idiom in the correct form.

keep a tight rein on someone
keep oneself to oneself
keep up appearances
keep something dark
keep in touch
keep someone posted

▷ Bill Parker didn't resign – he was fired! He didn't want anyone to know, so he _____ , but the truth gradually came out.
kept it dark

1 I'm moving to London next month, but I'll _____ . Here's my new address.

2 I'm very interested in any further developments. You will _____ , won't you?

3 I heard that Dick Doyle has gone bankrupt. If it's true, he certainly manages to _____ . He still drives his Rolls-Royce.

4 'Who lives in the old house on the hill?' 'A poet. He lives on his own and we hardly ever see him. He _____ .'

5 The Wilsons' teenage son is in trouble with the police. They ought to have _____ . It's too late now.

79 make (EI 172-3)

Complete the sentences by choosing the correct idiom.

▷ Can't we continue our argument later? People are listening. For goodness sake, don't _____ here!
make a bomb   make a move   make a scene
make a scene

1 Jerry likes organizing people, and since he's been put in charge of the department, he has really been _____ . No half-hour tea breaks are allowed now.
making himself at home   making his presence felt   making headway

2 Michael's doing very well in micro-electronics. He's published a lot of research work and has already _____ .
made the grade   made a name for himself   made light of it

3 The train's just leaving. You'll have to _____ . Run!
make a move   make a dash for it   make a go of it

4 I'm sorry I laughed. I know your problem's very serious. Please don't think I was _____ of it.
making mincemeat   making light   making heavy weather

5 I can't afford to buy a new coat this winter. I'll have to _____ with the one I have.
make amends   make myself at home   make do

80 play, pull (EI 174-5)

Explain the meaning of the idioms in *italics*.

▷ Joe Carter won't *play ball with you* unless you agree to split the profits fifty-fifty.
co-operate

1 I refuse to *play second fiddle* to my brother any longer. My opinion counts as much as his.
2 Norman's a very intelligent fellow. If he *plays his cards right*, he could become a partner in the firm before he's forty.
3 Chris has told her boss that she'll leave the firm if she doesn't get a pay rise. I think she's *playing with fire*, because the boss doesn't like to be put under pressure.
4 If everybody *pulls their weight*, we'll have the work finished by the end of the week.
5 Simon's used to *pulling strings* to get what he wants. If he didn't know so many influential people, he would never have reached the position he's in now.
6 If you intend to pass the exam, you'll have to *pull your socks up*. You've done no work at all for weeks.

81 Mixed verbs (EI 155-85)

Which idiom describes the situation in the picture? Make short sentences using the correct idiom from the list.
burn the midnight oil
catch someone in the act
compare notes
lay down the law
let oneself go
look daggers at someone
lose the thread of something
pip someone at the post
send someone packing
wait one's turn
work wonders

▷ **The injection will work wonders.**

1

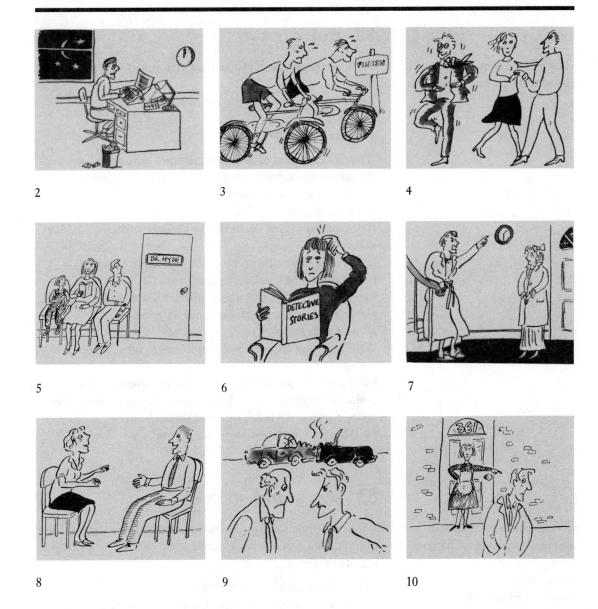

2

3

4

5

6

7

8

9

10

82 put (EI 175-7)

Complete the sentences by choosing the correct idiom.

▶ Victor obviously doesn't know what's happened. You had better _____ .
put him through his paces   *put him in his proper place*
put him in the picture
put him in the picture

1 'The bank has refused to extend the firm's loan, unless we change our marketing strategies.' 'Oh, I see. They are _____ .'
putting out their feelers   *putting the screws on us*
putting us through the mill

2 Jane slipped on some ice and broke her arm, so that _____ her skiing holiday.
put the skids under   *put the tin lid on*   *put the frighteners on*

3 Fred has been with us for over thirty years. In fact, it was Fred who actually _____ with a revolutionary new design.
put the firm on the map   *put the firm in the picture*
put paid to the firm

4 We've got some tricky technical problems to solve, so you had better _____ .
put your oar in   *put out your feelers*   *put your thinking cap on*

5 I think we ought to _____ . It was Margaret who proposed these policy changes, not Bill. The credit should be hers.
put the record straight   *put our house in order*
put someone on a pedestal

83 see, stand (EI 178-80)

Complete the sentences with the correct idiom in the correct form.
see the sights
stand one's ground
stand to lose something
see life
stand on ceremony
see reason
stand a fair chance

▶ If the prime minister handles the situation badly, he _____ a lot of votes in the forthcoming election.
stands to lose

1 'Why did you go to Rome?' 'Oh, just to _____ .'

2 I've explained to John a thousand times why leaving university now would be a wrong move, but he simply won't _____ .

3 Tessa has had six different jobs in ten different countries. She's been everything from a waitress to a tourist guide. She's certainly _____ .

4 I asked Ben's teacher if she thinks Ben ———— of getting a place at university. She's optimistic.
5 I overheard Anne having an argument with Chris. Chris is a good talker, but Anne is certainly able to ————.
6 'Should I wear a dinner-jacket on Saturday evening?' 'No, there's no need to ———— at the Langtons'. I'm sure some guests won't even be wearing a tie.'

84 take (EI 181-3)

Complete the sentences by choosing the correct idiom.

1 Mike and Phil had an argument last night about who does most cleaning in their flat. I was careful not to ————, as I want to stay good friends with them both.
take my pick   take the floor   take sides
2 Arthur has become very arrogant and over-confident since he won the election. He needs ————.
taking for a ride   taking amiss   taking down a peg
3 I'd prefer to go abroad instead of going into the family business, but I'm afraid my parents would ————.
take a dim view of it   take a rise out of me   take the plunge
4 People often ———— Alfred because he's so fat, but he never gets angry with them.
take advantage of   take the rap for   take a rise out of
5 I don't need these books any more. I'm giving them all away, so ————.
take pot luck   take them as read   take your pick
6 The garage charged Peter over a hundred pounds for repairs. I think he ————. In my opinion, the car only needed an oil change and new spark plugs.
was taken by storm   was taken to pieces   was taken for a ride
7 I think Jenny has been treated most unfairly, and if I were in her position, I wouldn't ————.
take the rough with the smooth   take it lying down
take it in my stride
8 What a nasty thing to say! I know Harry never has anything good to say about his colleagues, but this remark really ————!
takes the floor   takes its toll   takes the biscuit

9 'Don't you have some work to do in the kitchen?' 'All right. I can _____ . I'll leave you two alone.'
take a joke   take a hint   take the lid off something

10 Len was expecting to be asked to represent the company at the international congress in Geneva, so when Janet was asked to go instead, it really _____ .
took the wind out of his sails   took a leaf out of his book took him to the cleaners

85 throw, turn (EI 183-4)

Substitute for the phrase in *italics* an idiom from the list with the same meaning.

throw someone off his balance
throw in the towel
turn over a new leaf
turn up trumps
throw one's weight around
throw a fit
turn the corner

▶ When we tell the manageress that we are refusing to do overtime on Friday, she'll *become extremely angry*.
throw a fit

1 Steve used to be easy to work with, but since his promotion he's begun to *use his authority in an arrogant way*.

2 Karen was quite sure that she would be made head of department, but she wasn't. When the official announcement was made, it completely *confused her*. She was speechless.

3 This isn't the time to *stop trying*. You've failed the exam once, but you can take it again next year.

4 'How's your grandfather? Someone told me he had pneumonia.' 'Yes, we were very worried about him, but he has *passed the most critical part of it* now.'

5 Mick has been in trouble with the police a few times, but now he has promised his parents that he will *improve his behaviour and start again*.

6 I don't know how I would have overcome these difficulties without Sue. She *was a reliable friend* again as usual.

86 Mixed verbs (EI 155-85)

Complete the conversation with the correct idioms in the correct form.

be asking for trouble
be new to the game
blow one's own trumpet
call the shots
cross swords with someone
fly off the handle
know one's onions
pick holes in something
stick at nothing
tell someone where to get off

'Our new supervisor's not very popular with the office staff.'
    'Oh, why's that?
    'Well, she's the type who'll ___1___ to get what she wants.'
    '(She) ___2___ ?'
    'Yes. She isn't new to the firm, but she hasn't had a department to supervise before. But she obviously enjoys ___3___ and telling everyone what to do.'
    'How does she treat the staff?'
    'Well, she's already ___4___ several people's work, although the previous supervisor never had reason to be dissatisfied. And she's quite fond of ___5___ , telling us what a great person she is.'
    'It sounds to me as if she ___6___ . The staff won't stand that sort of treatment for long.'
    'You're right. Take old Henry, for instance. He's been with the firm for over thirty years and he really ___7___ . He's our best man. He won't take criticism that easily. If she ever ___8___ with him, he's likely to ___9___ and ___10___ . And we shall all support him!'

87 Mixed verbs (EI 155-85)

Complete the sentences with the correct idiom in the correct form.

bite off more than one can chew
bury the hatchet
call someone's bluff
clear the air
hold water
let someone off the hook
lose one's touch
meet one's match
pick a quarrel
ring a bell
rise to the occasion

▷ I wish Paul and Simon would forget about their old quarrel. It's time they _____ and became friends again.
buried the hatchet

1 Barbara's a very persuasive speaker, but when you examine her arguments, most of them are illogical. They simply don't _____ .
2 There's a lot of dissatisfaction in the department. The manager's going to call a meeting so that the staff can say what's troubling them. It's always a good idea to _____ .
3 Tom's afraid Pam won't have much time for him if she starts an Open University course, so he's threatened to break off their engagement. Pam simply ought to _____ , because she must know that he's not serious.
4 The last time I spoke to Jim he deliberately started to criticize my work. There was no real reason for it, he was just _____ .

5 'Do you remember Sheila Williams?' 'No, I don't. But the name _____ .'

6 I told my teacher that I can't do the French essay because I have to rehearse for the school play, so she said she would _____ until Monday.

7 Mr Barlow can't keep discipline in his classes as well as he used to. He thinks he's beginning to _____ .

8 Sue thought that she could manage a full-time job, but with three children it isn't as easy as she imagined. She admits that she has _____ .

9 Bob is an excellent golfer, but he's _____ in Richard, who's every bit as good.

10 I'm counting on you to run the department in my absence. I'm sure that you will _____ .

Idioms from special subjects

88 Banking (EI 186)

Complete the story with the correct idioms in the correct form.

draw money out
pay (money) in
make out a cheque
open an account
a crossed cheque
an open cheque
a current account
bounce
a deposit account
a joint account

I must tell you about a customer who came into the bank this morning – a strange old fellow, wearing a cap and a shabby raincoat. He said he wanted to ___1___ with our bank. From his questions, it sounded as if he had never had a bank account before, so I explained to him that with ___2___ you can ___3___ whenever you want, but with ___4___ you have to give a week's notice.

He seemed confused, so I showed him a cheque book and explained how to ___5___ – he had obviously never signed a cheque before. Then I explained the difference between ___6___ and ___7___. I also asked him if he wanted one signature on the cheque or whether it would be ___8___ together with his wife. He said he didn't want his wife to know anything about it! When I asked whether there would be regular payments into the account, he answered with a grin, 'Don't worry, my cheques won't ___9___, if that's what you're afraid of.'

Then he said he'd like to open a deposit account and brought out a parcel wrapped in newspaper. I tried not to look surprised when he opened it – it contained more than £10,000 tied up with string and rubber bands! 'That's just for a start,' he said. 'What I ___10___ tomorrow depends on how much I win on the horses today!'

89 Banking (EI 186)

Which is correct?

1 A 'blank cheque' has no _____ on it.
   date   signature   amount
2 When you write out a cheque, you are _____.
   the payee   the bearer   the drawer

3 One of the most common methods of payment
is _____ cheque.
with   through   by

4 A 'post-dated cheque' bears _____ .
a future date   a past date   a date that makes the cheque invalid

5 Your current account is 'in the red'. This means _____ .
you have no money in the account   you must mark your cheques R/D
you have money in the account

6 A 'bearer cheque' _____ .
can only be paid into an account   can be cashed by anyone who has it
bears the payee's name

90 Business *(EI 187)*

Which is correct?

1 If a business 'breaks even' it _____ .
ceases to exist   joins together with another company
makes neither profit nor loss

2 If a firm 'goes into liquidation' it _____ .
cannot pay its debts   offers shares to the general public
joins together with another firm

3 A 'board meeting' is _____ .
a meeting of a company's shareholders   a meeting of a company's staff
a meeting of a company's directors

4 A 'sleeping partner' is a person who _____ .
owns less than 50% of a company's capital   owns a dormant company
provides a percentage of a company's capital but takes no active part in
its management

5 'Sharp practices' are _____ .
fast business dealings   dishonest business dealings
fast and successful sales techniques

6 If you 'pull a fast deal', you _____ .
close a deal quickly   close a deal unfairly
refuse to close a deal quickly

91 Buying and selling (EI 187-8)

Complete the conversation with the correct idioms in the correct form.

on HP
out of stock
shop with someone
bring prices down
shop around
knock money off
sell like hot cakes
put prices up
do a roaring trade
take goods on approval

'Hello. Are you shopping here nowadays? Haven't I seen you in Sharp's a couple of times?'

'I'm just comparing prices.'

'Oh, I always do. It pays to __1__ . I used to __2__ Sharp's, but I don't buy much there now. This shop's much cheaper. They even let you __3__ so that you can decide at home whether or not to buy them. You can't do that at Sharp's. And here you can buy __4__ , on a monthly basis. You can't do that at Sharp's either. Mr Sharp does what he wants with his prices. He __5__ regularly, but he never __6__ . I bought a coffee-maker here last week. It had a small scratch on it, so they even __7__ . Sharp's wouldn't have done that. Mr Sharp is quite friendly, but they say his wife's very peculiar. Oh, look! Here are those new cheese graters. The shop assistant said they're __8__ and will soon be __9__ again, so I'll buy one now. Oh, just look at the queue at the check-out! This shop obviously __10__ . By the way, my name's Doreen Watson. What's yours?'

'Sharp!'

92 Health, illness, death (EI 189-90)

Complete the conversation with the correct idioms in the correct form.

run a temperature
on top of the world
come down with (an illness)
up to the mark
pass away
worn out
laid up
on the mend
throw off (an illness)
catch a cold

'Do you know that Mr Sykes has __1__ ? The funeral's on Friday. He was only fifty-five.'

'Yes, I heard. It was a sudden heart attack. Very sad. I saw him only last week and he said that apart from having a lot of work he was feeling __2__ . But I thought he looked tired, __3__ , in fact. But tell me, how's your husband?'

'Well, he __4__ a week ago and he doesn't seem able to __5__ (it). Several of his office colleagues have __6__ flu. He's __7__ as well, just over a hundred, so I called the doctor this morning. After all, I don't want him to be __8__ for Christmas.'

'No, of course not. My husband hasn't been feeling __9__ recently, either. Stomach trouble. But he must be __10__ now because he was shouting at the neighbour's cat again this morning as usual.'

93 Motoring (EI 190-1)

Complete the conversation with the correct idioms in the correct form.

jam on the brakes
the rush-hour
have a smash
back out
be stuck in a traffic jam
pull in
run into something
a write-off

'Hello, darling. Have you had a good day in town? I've been lying in the garden all day enjoying the sunshine.'

'No, I haven't had a good day. I've ___1___ with the car.'

'Oh, dear! Are you all right?'

'Yes, I'm all right, but the car isn't. It's not ___2___ but the repairs will come to at least five hundred pounds.'

'But what happened?'

'Well, you see, it was around five o'clock. ___3___ was in full swing, cars and buses everywhere. I had already ___4___ for over half an hour. I remembered that I'd forgotten to go to the baker's, so I looked for somewhere to park. I saw a small space in front of an entrance to a yard. There was a "No parking" sign, but I didn't think it would matter for just a few minutes. So I ___5___ . I bought the bread, hopped back into the car and was just ___6___ when suddenly a huge delivery van appeared behind me! We both ___7___ , but he couldn't stop in time, so he ___8___ me, of course. He was annoyed and started shouting the usual rubbish about women drivers.'

'So your poor little Mini's had quite a day!'

'Well, the thing is – er – when I went into the garage this morning I couldn't start *my* car – so I'm afraid it was *your* car I was driving.'

94 Politics and government (EI 191-2)

Which is correct?

1   A candidate for election _____ or _____ .
stands for office   goes for office   sits for office   runs for office

2   A 'maiden speech' is made in the House _____ .
by female MPs   by new MPs   only by ministers

3   'Front benchers' are _____ .
seats at the front of the House
long-serving members of parliament
members of parliament who hold ministerial office

4   If the Prime Minister 'goes to the country', he or she _____ .
resigns   holds a referendum   calls a general election

5 In politics, the adjective 'shadow' means _____ .
of the governing party   of the opposition party   previous
second in importance

95 The Stock Exchange (EI 192)

Which is correct?

1 A 'bull market' means that _____ .
share prices are rising   share prices are falling
share prices are not moving
2 A 'bear market' means that _____ .
share prices are rising   share prices are falling
share prices are not moving
3 'Blue chips' are _____ .
securities issued by the government
industrial shares considered to be a safe investment
industrial shares considered to be a risky investment
4 'Gilt-edged securities' are _____ .
shares which pay high dividends   new share issues
shares issued by the government
5 If shares are 'at par', they sell at _____ .
their nominal value, i.e. their original price   the market value
their lowest price ever

96 Telephoning (EI 193-4)

Complete the conversation with the correct idioms in the correct form.
a crossed line
go dead
be cut off
put someone through
take the call
hold the line
out of order
get through
ring off
the line is engaged

'I've been trying to ring my brother Nick at work, but I couldn't __1__ to him. First of all, it took me half an hour to find a phone-box that worked – the first three I went into were all __2__ . I dialled Nick's number and heard it ringing, then there was silence, nothing! The line had simply __3__ . I dialled again and got a wrong number. The third time, Nick must have been phoning someone himself because __4__ . At the fourth try I had __5__ – I could hear two people having a rather personal conversation. The fifth time, I managed to speak to Nick's secretary. I asked her to __6__ to Nick. She told me to __7__ and I heard her ask Nick if he wanted to __8__ . Of course he said "Yes" and we exchanged a few words, then for some reason we __9__ and we lost the connection. By this time

I was very angry. I dialled a sixth time, but it was a bad line, so I had to __10__ . When I tried again later, the secretary told me Nick had left the office for the afternoon!'

'How annoying! But tell me, what was it that you wanted to tell your brother so urgently?'

'That my home telephone's out of order! Nick is the head of the fault section at British Telecom.'

97 Travel (EI 194)

Complete the dialogues with the correct words from the list, changing the form where necessary. Use some words twice.

off
up
on
over
in
by
do
make
take

1 'Last Sunday we went _____ a trip to Lake Windermere.'
'How did you go? _____ coach or _____ car?'
2 'Are you going _____ holiday this year?'
'Yes, my wife would like to _____ a cruise, so it won't be a cheap holiday, I'm afraid.'
3 'What time did you set _____ when you went to Edinburgh?'
'Not until lunch-time, so we had to stop _____ in the Lake District on the way.'
4 'Did you put _____ at a hotel?'
'Yes, but since we hadn't _____ a reservation, we had difficulty getting a room.'
5 'The flight leaves at nine forty-five, so what time should we check _____ ?'
'Not later than nine. Remember, we've got a lot of luggage to weigh _____ .'
6 'What are you doing next weekend?'
'We're going on a short break holiday to Paris. I haven't been there before, so I'm looking forward to _____ the sights.'

98 Work and industrial relations
(EI 194-6)

Which is correct?

1 Which of the following is not a form of worker protest?
a go-slow   a work-to-rule   a lock-out
2 Workers 'on the shop floor' are _____ .
shop assistants   shop stewards
manual workers on the production line

3 Which three mean the same?
  a shop steward   a blackleg   a strike breaker   a scab   a picket
4 Which two expressions mean 'finish work for the day'?
  knock off   lay off   sign off   clock off
5 When a worker is 'laid off' he _____.
  is ill   is out of work temporarily   is out of work permanently
6 If you work longer than your usual working hours, you _____.
  work unsocial hours   do overtime   do shift-work
7 An unemployed person receiving money from the state is said to be _____.
  on the board   on the shop floor   on the dole
8 If you apply for a job but are not accepted you are _____.
  laid off   made redundant   turned down

Idioms with key words from special categories

Animals

99 Animals (EI 197-203)

Complete the sentences with the correct idiom in the correct form.

have a bee in one's bonnet
take the bull by the horns
have butterflies in one's stomach
let the cat out of the bag
not stand a cat in hell's chance
go to the dogs
barking dogs seldom bite
do the donkey work
cook someone's goose
hold one's horses
smell a rat

▶ Tom's report is excellent, but remember that it was his assistant who ＿＿＿, compiling facts and figures from miles of computer print-out.
did the donkey work

1 My Uncle Bert lives on health food. He ＿＿＿ about living to be a hundred, and he won't eat anything that contains animal fat.

2 'How did you find out about the party?' 'Well, it was Jeff who ＿＿＿. I suppose he thought I knew about it.'

3 The roof's fallen in, the floors are rotting and the garden's run wild. What a pity to let such a lovely old house ＿＿＿ like that.

4 Mike was hoping to spend the weekend alone with Joan, fishing in Scotland. But then Joan's brother arrived unexpectedly, so they had to take him with them. Poor old Mike. That really ＿＿＿.

5 'Do you think Rod will get the job that he applied for?' 'No, in my opinion he ＿＿＿. He simply isn't good enough.'

6 Oh dear – I'm beginning to get nervous now. I always ＿＿＿ before an exam. Don't you?

7 Old Mr Fletcher is always complaining about the children making a noise and kicking their football into his garden. He's threatened to call the police, but I'm sure he won't. ＿＿＿.

8 'Will you let me drive your new car?' '＿＿＿! I've only just ordered it. I won't get it until January at the earliest.'

9 After their quarrel, Pamela and Jack avoided each other for weeks, until Jack decided to ＿＿＿ and invite Pamela to a concert. Now they're good friends again.

10 I'm surprised that Greg didn't sense that something was wrong. In his position, I think I would have ＿＿＿.

100 Animals (EI 197-203)

Which idiom describes the
picture? Complete the
sentences using idioms which
include the words in the list.
whale
cat
cats and dogs
snail
crocodile
beast
lark

1 It's _____.

2 She's having a _____.

▶ The children are having
_____.

a whale of a time

3 She's crying _____.

4 Every morning he's _____.

5 Johnny is _____ of himself
again.

6 The traffic's going _____.

Colours

101 Colours (EI 203-6)

Complete the sentences by choosing the correct word from the list. Use one word twice.

blue
black
red
green

▷ I've paid off my overdraft at last! I must admit that I feel better now that I'm *in the* _____ *again.*
black

1 I got a letter this morning saying that an uncle in Australia had left me some money in his will. I didn't know that I still had an uncle in Australia, so it was completely *out of the* _____ .

2 It isn't all that easy to get a visa and work permit for the States. There's still a lot of _____ *tape.*

3 Don't believe all the bad things you've heard about Tom Spencer. He isn't *as* _____ *as he is painted.*

4 The plans are ready, so as soon as you *give me the* _____ *light* I'll start with the construction work.

5 'Do you still visit your friends in Edinburgh?' 'No, not since we moved to Cambridge. Only *once in a* _____ *moon,* unfortunately.'

102 Colours (EI 203-6)

Complete the sentences by choosing the correct idiom.

1 'What did you think of the Prime Minister's speech?' 'Too many _____ . She was trying to divert attention away from the really important issues.'
white lies   black sheep   red herrings

2 Tina came home and announced to her parents that she had got engaged to Frank. It was _____ for them, because they hadn't even met him!
a red letter day   a black mark   a bolt from the blue

3 'Some of the new plants in my garden don't seem to be growing very well.' 'Well, ask Ted what to do about them. He's got _____ .'
red tape   green fingers   grey matter   a green belt

4 Matthew and Walter are both highly respectable lawyers. It's Simon who's the _____ . He went off to Mexico with a night-club dancer.
blue-eyed boy   black mark   black sheep

5 If you see Robert, don't mention me. I'm afraid I was very rude
to him last night, so now I'm ____ .
in the black   in the red   in his black books   in a blue funk

Numbers, size, measurement

103 number (EI 207)

Explain the meaning of the
idioms in *italics*.

▷ Who's Alekseev's *opposite number* in the British Government?
person occupying the same position

1 Paul only thinks about *number one*. He doesn't consider the
feelings of others at all.
2 I wanted to speak to Mrs Marsden but apparently she's on a
business trip. Who's her *number two*?
3 Whoever called Charles Thorpe *a back number* is badly informed.
Charles still has considerable influence in the company.
4 When the Prime Minister finds out that it was Archer who
leaked the confidential report his *number will be up*.
5 I've promised my mother that when my *number comes up* I'll buy
her a cottage in the country.

104 one (EI 207-9)

Substitute for the phrase in
italics an idiom from the list with
the same meaning.
one of these days
be one up on someone
one in the eye for someone
back to square one
one by one
one too many
one or two

▷ The project has used up all the money and hasn't brought the
expected results, so unfortunately we're *back where we started*.
back to square one

1 It will be *a nasty shock to* Jim when he hears that Paul has been
chosen to head the teaching team instead of him.
2 The club president first addressed the group. Then he thanked
the members *individually*.
3 I'll ring for a taxi to take Alex home. In my opinion he's had *too
much to drink*.
4 John sometimes cheats in maths tests. His teacher hasn't
caught him yet, but *before long* she will!
5 I was lucky at the interview. I *had an advantage over* most of the
other candidates because of my fluent Spanish.
6 'Can you lend me some coins for the phone-box?' 'Sorry, I
can't. I've only got *a few* and I need them myself.'

105 two, three, etc. (EI 209-12)

Which idiom describes the picture? Complete the sentences with the correct idiom in the correct form.

be in two minds about something
two heads are better than one
two's company
three cheers for someone!
on all fours
knock someone for six
at sixes and sevens
dressed up to the nines
on cloud nine
nineteen to the dozen
forty winks

1 He's _____ looking for his spectacles.

2 Someone has _____ .

3 She _____ about going to the party.

4 _____ for Harry!

▶ He's taking _____ .
forty winks

5 They've been chatting _____ for hours!

6 Aunt Maggie was _____ .

7 They're thinking
that _____ .

8 They agree that _____ .

9 She's had some good news.
She's _____ .

10 Uncle Bob was _____ .

106 size, inch, mile (EI 212-13)

Explain the meaning of the
idioms in *italics*.

▷ So *that's about the size of it*. I've given you all the facts and now
the matter's in your hands.
that's a fair description of the situation

1 The new cook has only been here two weeks, but she's already
behaving as if the canteen couldn't be run without her. It's time
someone *cut her down to size*.

2 Don't imagine that I'm going to buy this Rolls-Royce – I'm not
that rich. I'm just sitting at the wheel and *trying it for size*!

3 I was *within an inch of* resigning today. I had a serious difference
of opinion with my head of department.

4 Patrick not only has a typically Irish sense of humour. He's *every
inch* an Irishman.

5 We tried to persuade Greg to change his decision, but he wouldn't *budge an inch*.
6 Were you speaking to me? Sorry, I was *miles away*.
7 Robert says it doesn't matter that he didn't get the scholarship, but you can *see his disappointment a mile off*.
8 One of the new trainees is especially bright and quick to learn, but she also *talks a mile a minute*.

Parts of the body

107 arm, back, blood, bone (EI 213-15)

Complete the sentences with the correct idiom in the correct form.

give one's right arm
keep someone at arm's length
with open arms
behind someone's back
see the back of something
put someone's back up
put one's back into something
get someone's blood up
be in someone's blood
make no bones about something
have got a bone to pick with someone

▷ I wish Barry would stop bragging about his football successes. His arrogance really _____ .
   puts my back up

1 'Didn't Jim tell his wife that he'd decided to sell the car?' 'No, that's what the big quarrel was about. He did it _____ .'
2 The fellow in the flat above always wastes my time chatting, so I try to _____ .
3 You are so lucky to get the chance of going to work in Japan. I'd _____ to be asked to go.
4 This report is extremely time consuming. I'll be glad to _____ .
5 Music must _____ . She could play the piano and the violin beautifully at the age of six.
6 I'll _____ . I thought the way you handled the situation was inadequate, to say the least.
7 We're behind schedule with production. If we still intend to get the order out before the end of the month, we'll have to _____ .
8 Don't go away. I _____ you. Why did you tell Sue that I don't like her new car? I told you that in confidence.
9 Why are some people so greedy? That kind of behaviour really _____ .
10 The children loved the old train set you found in your attic. They welcomed it _____ .

108 brain, chest, ear, elbow (EI 215-17)

Complete the sentences by choosing the correct idiom.

▷ Mary has some very good ideas for English conversation classes. Why don't you _____ before your new course begins?
rack her brain   pick her brain   keep your ear to the ground
pick her brain

1 We've got a new junior assistant, fresh from law school. He's very idealistic – still _____ .
out on his ear   all ears   wet behind the ears

2 If you want the wood to really shine, you'll have to put a bit more _____ into it!
elbow room   elbow grease   brain drain

3 I'm sorry, but I really haven't got time to come with you. You can see that I'm _____ .
all ears   out on my ear   up to my ears

4 Roger hasn't decided just how much to tell Jack about the new situation. He's going to wait for Jack's reaction first and then _____ .
play by ear   play it by ear   keep his ear close to the ground

5 I've decided to tell Nicole that it was my mistake. She'll find out the truth herself before long, so I'd rather _____ now.
*turn a deaf ear to it   play my cards close to my chest
get it off my chest*

6 'Have you found those files yet?' 'No, I've been _____ for hours but I can't remember where I left them.'
having a brainwave   racking my brains   picking my brains

109 eye (EI 217-19)

Which idiom describes the picture? Complete the sentences with the correct idiom in the correct form.

see eye to eye
be up to the eyes
pull the wool over someone's eyes
cry one's eyes out
turn a blind eye to something
catch someone's eye
keep one's eyes peeled

1 He's _____ in work.

2 She's _____ .

▷ He couldn't _____ .
pull the wool over the judge's eyes

3 They don't _____ .

4 She's trying to _____ .

5 He's _____ .

6 He's _____ the dirty dishes.

110 face, finger (EI 219-21)

Substitute for the phrase in *italics* an idiom from the list with the same meaning.

put a brave face on it
lose face
face the music
let's face it
be staring someone in the face
all fingers and thumbs
keep one's fingers crossed
put one's finger on something
have got a finger in every pie

▶ If you really don't want to *be humiliated* in the office, admit your mistake and apologize to the rest of the staff.
lose face

1 Rob is very worried about his wife's condition, but for the sake of the children, he's *pretending nothing is seriously wrong*.

2 I know that selling the house will be a hard blow to us all, but *let's be truthful*, we need the money.

3 Surely you can see what he wants. *It's very obvious*. He's going to ask you to marry him!

4 Well, Paul, it was your fault and you'll have to *meet the criticism and unpleasantness* some time. So why not now?

5 I'm going for an important interview this afternoon at three, so *wish me luck*!

6 Brewer *is involved in many activities*. He's on every local committee you can mention.

7 Oh, I'm so sorry. I've dropped all your books. I'm *clumsy with my hands* today, I'm afraid.

8 There's something about the way Jason looks at me that makes me feel uneasy, but I can't *identify it*.

111 foot, feet, hair (EI 221-2)

Complete the sentences with the correct idiom in the correct form.

fall on one's feet
get off on the wrong foot
put one's best foot forward
put one's foot in it
get back on one's feet
put one's foot down
let one's hair down
not turn a hair
keep your hair on!

▶ Would you believe it! The day after Dave resigned, he had a phone call from Tokyo offering him a job at twice his present salary! Dave always _____ .
falls on his feet

1 Father's easygoing and tolerant, but he _____ when Mike asked him if twelve of his friends could camp in the living-room after the party. That was simply too much to ask.

2 I didn't know that Joan and Barry had separated. I'm afraid I _____ when I asked Joan why Barry was away from home so often.

3 If you intend to finish the decorating by this evening, you'll have to _____ . The kitchen will take longer than you think.

4 Jackie and I have never really liked each other. For some reason we _____ because of a misunderstanding, and we never really became friends.

5 When Helen had to close her restaurant she lost quite a lot of money, but it didn't take her long to _____ .

6 Thorpe was unmoved by the verdict. When the jury pronounced him guilty, he _____ .

7 All right! _____ . If it makes you angry I won't do it!

8 When the formalities are over we shall all be able to _____ and have a really good time.

112 hand (EI 222-5)

Complete the sentences by choosing the correct idiom.

1 Bob would repair your car for you. He used to work as a car mechanic and he likes to _____ by doing small repair jobs.
   strengthen his hand   keep his hand in   show his hand

2 'Can you tell me Joe's new telephone number?' 'No, not _____ . But I've got it written down somewhere.'
   at hand   to hand   off hand   hands off

3 'Who told you that Jane and Patrick are moving to Exeter?' 'I found out _____ . Jane told me herself.'
   at hand   at first hand   off hand   in hand

4 I asked Mary if she had time to help with the exhibition, but she says she _____ already.
   *is putting her hand to the plough   has her hands full
   is forcing her hand*

5 I need some help with these boxes. Could you possibly _____ ?
   give me a big hand   give me a free hand   give me a hand

6 The new product was a failure and the firm lost orders _____ .
   cap in hand   hand over fist   out of hand

113 head (EI 225-6)

Explain the meaning of the idioms in *italics*.

▷ I was so upset when the accident happened. I don't know how I managed to *keep my head*.
   stay calm

1 Janet has *got it into her head* that she's not as physically fit as she ought to be, so she's joined a health club.

2   I'm afraid I don't know much about computers, so what you're saying is *above my head*.

3   Sally has always *had a good head for figures*. She'd like to become an accountant.

4   Can you *make head or tail of* Uncle Ken's letter? I can't. Is he coming next week or isn't he?

5   If you haven't got much time, don't visit Mr Green today. He'll *talk your head off*!

6   Dave, stop *talking through the back of your head*! What you're saying is untrue and quite impossible.

114 heart, heel, leg (EI 226-8)

Which idiom describes the picture? Complete the sentences by choosing the correct idiom.

1   Tom's doing his homework but _____ .
his heart's in his mouth
his heart isn't in it
he hasn't the heart

2   He's trying to learn the formulas _____ .
at heart
to his heart's content
by heart

3   He's beginning to _____ .
take heart
lose heart
break his heart

4   Someone criticized her and she's _____ .
taken it to heart
broken her heart
set her heart on it

5 When the police arrived, the
thieves _____ .
were down at heel
kicked their heels
took to their heels

6 His car _____ .
doesn't have a leg to stand on
is on its last legs
needs a leg up

115   neck (EI 228-9)

What's missing? Complete the
sentences using an idiom from
the list in the correct form.
be neck and neck
be up to the neck in something
break one's neck
breathe down someone's neck
get it in the neck

1 He'll _____ when his
mother sees what he's done.

2 He fell down the steps and
almost _____ .

3 She _____ in work.

4 The runners _____ right up
to the finishing line.

5 I wish she'd stop _____ !

116 nose, shoulder (EI 229)

Complete the sentences with the correct idiom in the correct form.

keep one's nose to the grindstone
lead someone by the nose
pay through the nose
turn one's nose up at something
give someone the cold shoulder
rub shoulders with someone
put one's shoulder to the wheel

▷ You obviously don't think the quality of the material is good enough. I can see that you're ____ .
turning your nose up at it

1 I can't believe that this painting is so valuable. I hope we haven't ____ for it.
2 The workers were very angry because they felt that the union leaders were ____ .
3 You have obviously been working very hard. If you ____ you should have the report finished by this afternoon.
4 You can't expect to pass the exam without doing any work. It's time you ____ , before it's too late.
5 Why didn't Hilary speak to me? Didn't she see me or was she deliberately ____ ?
6 When John was in the diplomatic service, he often used to ____ members of the royal family.

117 skin, toe (EI 230)

Substitute for the phrase in *italics* an idiom from the list with the same meaning.

drenched to the skin
get under someone's skin
by the skin of one's teeth
tread on someone's toes
toe the line
be on one's toes
be no skin off someone's nose

▷ If I were you, I wouldn't worry about Clive. It *won't affect you adversely* whether he makes a success of his new business or not.
will be no skin off your nose

1 The diver said that sharks had been following him and that he had only escaped *very narrowly*.
2 I picked Marjorie up at the bus-stop. Poor thing, she was *thoroughly wet*.
3 Mike is always criticizing without reason. He really *annoys me*.
4 You have to *be alert and attentive* when you're driving through the city centre in the rush-hour.
5 Parker always expects us to *do what he wants*. He forgets that we have opinions and ideas of our own.
6 I didn't know that Sarah had baked the cake herself. I'm afraid I *hurt her feelings* when I said that cream cakes are bad for you.

118 tongue, tooth, teeth (EI 230-1)

Complete the sentences with the correct idiom in the correct form.

have something on the tip of one's tongue
hold one's tongue
bite one's tongue off
have got a sweet tooth
fight tooth and nail
cut one's teeth on something
get one's teeth into something

▷ He asked me the name of the shop. I _____ but I didn't remember it until he'd gone.
   had it on the tip of my tongue

1 There are times when it's wiser to _____ than to say what one thinks.

2 'How do you manage to keep so slim?' 'Well, I (not) _____ , so it isn't really difficult.'

3 I thought Paul knew that Sarah had gone to Glasgow with Mark. I could have _____ when I realized that he didn't. How tactless of me to mention it!

4 Bill would like me to give him an easy computer programme to write. He did well on the programming course, so now he needs something to _____ .

5 We're all against the plans for the new motorway and local politicians are prepared to _____ to get them stopped.

6 The job seemed difficult at first, but as soon as I _____ it, I realized that it wasn't so bad after all.

Time

119 day (EI 231-3)

Complete the sentences by choosing the correct idiom.

1 It's late. We ought to _____ and continue with the work tomorrow.
   make a day of it   make our day   call it a day

2 It's twenty years _____ that we came to live here.
   the other day   to the day   this day week

3 Mother had a telephone call from my brother in Australia this morning. She was very pleased, of course. It really _____ .
   made her day   was her day   won the day

4 We visited Sheila this morning and she suggested _____ and staying for lunch and afternoon tea. So we did.
   having a field day   calling it a day   making a day of it

5 The language course was excellent. I found that my English improved _____ .
   day in day out   to a day   day by day

120 hour, minute, moment, night

(EI 233-4)

Complete the conversation with the correct idioms in the correct form.

keep regular hours
an unearthly hour
the small hours
a night owl
have a night out
at any moment
have one's moments
have a minute to call one's own
a night on the town
on the spur of the moment

'Morning, Paul! You look tired.'

'Yes, I am. I had a late night last night. I'm not usually ___1___, but I ___2___ with some friends yesterday. I've been so busy all week that I've hardly ___3___, so I really enjoyed ___4___. I start work early, so I usually ___5___, but yesterday was an exception. I didn't come home until ___6___. It was about two thirty, I think. I got into bed and must have fallen asleep, because the next thing I knew my landlady was shaking me, saying she was sorry to wake me at such ___7___, but she thought there was a burglar in the kitchen. She had heard noises and wanted me to take a look.'

'Well, where was her husband?'

'Mr Pearson's working on the night-shift, and since their son's on holiday I was the only man in the house. I'm usually a coward, but I do ___8___, so I grabbed my tennis racket, which was the only thing I could think of ___9___, and crept downstairs.'

'And then?'

'I saw a dark figure in the kitchen with a knife in his hand, ready to strike ___10___. I was just about to hit him with the racket when a voice shouted out, "Hey! It's me!" It was Mr Pearson. He had forgotten his sandwiches.'

121 time (EI 234-6)

Complete the sentences by choosing the correct idiom.

➤ That clock is unreliable. It's been _____ recently.
behind the times   keeping bad time   taking its time
keeping bad time

1 If you want to make a really good job of laying the carpet, you'll have to _____ .
take your time   bide your time   keep good time

2 I've asked Mike _____ not to leave his car in front of my gates, but he always forgets.
time and again   at times   in the nick of time

3 I'm sorry I can't stop for a chat, but I'm _____ at the moment.
behind the times   in no time   pressed for time   buying time

4 'What's Sarah doing these days?' 'She's starting college in October, so _____ she's helping her father in the shop.'
from time to time   for the time being   at times

5 'It's December already. This year has passed so quickly.' 'Indeed, _____.'
time's up   there's no time like the present   time flies

6 Sorry I'm late. Am I still _____ for some coffee or has it all gone?
in the nick of time   on time   in time   at the time

7 The police thought Jerry McGregor was behind the bank robbery, until they realized that he was still _____.
biding time   doing time   having the time of his life

8 I arrived late at the station and almost missed my train. I just managed to jump on it _____.
at the best of times   in no time   in the nick of time

9 Jim's very good and quick at repairing things. He'll fix your leaking tap _____.
in good time   in no time   in his own good time

10 Penny's waiting for a vacancy in the legal department. Until then, she's _____ in the sales department.
doing time   playing for time   biding her time

Idioms with comparisons

122 Comparisons with *as . . . as*

(EI 237-8)

Which comparison describes the picture? Use an adjective and a noun from the lists.

cold	mud
brown	ice
black	post
fit	coal
clear	Punch
pleased	fiddle
deaf	berry

1 The room's ＿＿.

2 Grandad's ＿＿.

▶ He's ＿＿.
as brown as a berry

3 She's ＿＿.

4 The doctor says he's ＿＿.

5　His hands and face are ＿＿.

6　The explanation is ＿＿.

123　Comparisons with *as . . . as*
(EI 237-8)

Complete the sentences with a comparison, using an adjective and a noun from the lists.

old	*daisy*
warm	*lightning*
quick	*leather*
white	*toast*
tough	*sheet*
quiet	*mouse*
fresh	*hills*

▶ I promise not to disturb you. I'll just sit here and I'll be ＿＿. **as quiet as a mouse**

1　After a good night's sleep you'll feel ＿＿.

2　I'm ＿＿ in these new boots. Look how thick the fur lining is!

3　Quickly! Find a chair for this patient, nurse. He's ＿＿ and I think he's going to faint.

4　I'm afraid the meal I cooked was a disaster. It took so long to cut and chew the steak. It was ＿＿.

5　Pam's very good at adding up figures. I always need a calculator, but she's ＿＿.

6　'Have you heard the news about Kevin's skiing holiday?' 'Oh, you mean when he broke his leg on the airport escalator and spent his holiday in a Munich hospital? That story's ＿＿.'

124 Comparisons with *like* (EI 238-41)

Which comparison with *like* describes the picture? Use a verb and a noun from the lists.

go	chimney
look	bomb
run	drowned rat
sing	hare
sleep	water
smoke	log
spend money	lark

1 Tim can ____ .

2 Uncle Ken ____ .

▶ Fred's new car ____ .
goes like a bomb

3 His wife ____ .

4 She ____ .

5 She's in her chair, ____ .

6 She was standing in the rain, ____ .

125 Comparisons with *like* (EI 238-41)

Complete the sentences with a comparison with *like*, using a verb and a noun from the lists.

fit	*leaf*
drink	*horse*
eat	*wildfire*
treat	*dirt*
grin	*fish*
spread	*Cheshire cat*
shake	*glove*

▶ I think I'll buy these jeans. They're perfect. They _____.
fit like a glove

1 'Last night in the pub Jim Spence was ordering pints of bitter as if they were glasses of water.' 'Yes, I know. He _____.'

2 What's wrong with Sally? Has she had a shock? She's _____.

3 I've never seen anyone eat as much food as Patrick does. He _____.

4 Someone told me that it's very unpleasant working for that firm. They _____ their employees _____.

5 The news that Mr Chamberlain was resigning _____. Everyone knew about it an hour after he had told the Managing Director.

6 Why are you _____? What do you find so amusing?

Key

1

1 am in her bad books   2 a bad lot   3 is going from bad to worse   4 a bad patch   5 make the best of a bad job

2

1 a big hit   2 in a big way   3 a big noise 4 gave her a big hand   5 make it big

3

1 a dead end   2 cut me dead   3 dead right 4 a dead loss   5 made a dead set at

4

1 and that's flat   2 told him flat   3 fell flat 4 knocked me flat   5 in two minutes flat

5

1 do you good   2 be as good as gold   3 Have a good time   4 be for good   5 do you a good turn

6

1 hard hit   2 a hard and fast rule   3 hard cash 4 playing hard to get   5 hard up

7

1 been in high spirits   2 high and low   3 get on his high horse   4 be for the high jump   5 high and dry

8

1 a hot spot   2 are very knowledgeable about it 3 are undecided   4 make things difficult for him 5 hot under the collar

9

1 the truth   2 a guess   3 be successful 4 in planning for the distant future   5 the same whatever you do

10

1 an old fogey   2 the old man   3 an old hand 4 a chip off the old block   5 an old flame

11

1 run short   2 for short   3 fell short of 4 short and to the point   5 little short of

12

1 thin on top   2 laying it on thick   3 in the thick of it   4 as thin as a rake   5 as thick as thieves

13

1 went off at the deep end   2 got hold of the wrong end of the stick   3 in the end   4 to no end 5 at the end of the day

14

1 take the line of least resistance   2 right down the line   3 Somewhere along the line   4 fall into line with   5 get a line on

15

1 a matter of life and death   2 no matter who 3 a matter of opinion   4 no laughing matter 5 a matter of time

16

1 I feel almost sure that I am going to   2 take a decision   3 I feel inclined   4 have many things to think about   5 said openly what you think

17

1 stretch a point   2 Get to the point   3 see the point of   4 what's the point?   5 in point of fact

18

1 a near thing   2 Sure thing!   3 not quite the thing 4 just the thing   5 just one of those things

19

1 have her own way   2 have it both ways   3 mend his ways   4 has a way with   5 go his own way

20

1 take his word for it   2 word for word   3 have a word   4 has the last word   5 mum's the word

21

1 improve her financial and social standing
2 wonderful   3 lost her financial and social position   4 in a very happy mood   5 very different from each other

22

1 he is very tired   2 he is clever and alert   3 is very popular   4 doesn't care at all   5 at least £2000

23

1 how about   2 and how!   3 How come
4 How on earth   5 How's it going

24

1 it is very surprising   2 I can't understand
3 it's not possible to predict what will happen
4 it does not matter   5 it is a just punishment

25

1 step on it   2 been at it   3 catch it   4 Jump to it!
5 take it easy   6 hold it!   7 Take it or leave it
8 Blast it!   9 out with it   10 sleep on it

26

1 That's the ticket   2 Come to that   3 That will do
4 That does it!   5 That's torn it!

27

1 there's nothing difficult involved   2 straight away
3 there is no other way   4 I don't know the answer
5 one can't know what will happen

28

1 too much of a good thing   2 too many cooks
3 too good to be true   4 too big for his boots
5 too true!

29

1 has got what it takes   2 What's the game?
3 and what's more   4 and what not
5 knows what's what

30

1 castles in the air   2 a flash in the pan   3 a turn-up for the books   4 a spoke in his wheel   5 a bit on the side

31

1 a blessing in disguise   2 a cog in the machine
3 a mug's game   4 a feather in his cap
5 another cup of tea   6 a pillar of society
7 the gift of the gab   8 the tricks of the trade
9 a piece of cake   10 his own man

32

1 a tough customer   2 a tight squeeze   3 a flash Harry   4 a square peg   5 a close thing

33

1 a flying visit   2 a confirmed bachelor   3 a bitter pill   4 a soft spot   5 a blind date   6 a live wire
7 a snap decision   8 a down payment   9 a going concern   10 plain sailing

34

1 a rolling stone   2 an open secret   3 an inside job
4 a close thing   5 a wet blanket

35

1 cut and dried   2 bright and breezy   3 spick and span   4 free and easy   5 hale and hearty

36

1 hammer and tongs   2 peace and quiet
3 rack and ruin   4 touch and go   5 ins and outs

37

1 occasionally   2 practically   3 seldom
4 not important   5 at irregular intervals

38

1 pick and choose   2 wait and see   3 grin and bear it   4 tossed and turned   5 give and take

39

1 bit by bit   2 again and again   3 by and by
4 blow by blow   5 all in all

40

1 Yes, it will go *against the grain*.   2 Yes, it was
completely *above board*.   3 Yes, he's cleaned it *after a
fashion*.   4 Yes, it goes *across the board*.   5 Yes, he's
feeling *above par*.

41

1 in a state of disagreement   2 if absolutely
necessary   3 haphazardly   4 always and
everywhere   5 without a break

42

1 behind the scenes   2 below par   3 by leaps and
bounds   4 behind closed doors   5 by degrees

43

1 Yes, I read it *from cover to cover*.   2 Yes, it's his *for
the asking*.   3 Yes, they did it just *for kicks*.
4 No, he only said it *for fun*.   5 No, she learnt it *from
scratch*.

44

1 in the dumps   2 in the flesh   3 in stitches
4 in trim   5 in a stew

45

1 off the beaten track   2 off the peg   3 off colour
4 off the record   5 off form

46

1 on the off-chance   2 On balance   3 on call
4 on the beat   5 on the run   6 on the move
7 on the dole   8 on the dot   9 on the rack
10 on the tiles

47

1 out of condition/out of the running   2 out of
place   3 out for the count   4 out of sorts
5 over the moon

48

1 mad   2 in every way   3 up to the present time
4 exactly   5 without help   6 receiving medical
treatment   7 secret   8 out of her senses
9 exactly the thing he enjoys   10 not more than we
can afford

49

1 is in for   2 be down on   3 be on to   4 be up
against   5 was into

50

1 break up   2 broke it up   3 break her in
4 bringing in   5 brought off   6 brought it on

51

1 calls for   2 called on   3 carry on   4 catch on
5 catch up   6 call in

52

1 came up   2 coming along   3 came across
4 came to   5 coming in

53

1 drive sharply in front of you   2 reduced her
consumption of   3 upset   4 fasten   5 prevent you
from getting it   6 need

54

1 got through   2 got over   3 get by   4 get down
to   5 is getting on   6 get up to   7 get away with it
8 get off   9 get out of   10 got up

55

1 gone off   2 go for   3 go through with it
4 go for me   5 going on   6 gone up
7 going through   8 go into

56

1 wait   2 keep   3 stand waiting   4 teasing you
5 discuss it fully with her   6 have an engagement

57

1 hold with   2 hold out   3 hold out for
4 hold over   5 holds off

58

1 kept at it   2 Keep on   3 kept you up   4 keep in
5 Keep out of   6 keep up with

59

1 over   2 on   3 down   4 up   5 into   6 in
7 out   8 to

60

1 make out   2 making things up   3 made off
4 make it out   5 made over   6 made for
7 make off with   8 make up for

61

1 Yes, she just *passed out*.   2 No, they *played it down*.
3 Yes, it has *passed off*.   4 No, I'll have to *pass on it*.
5 No, it's *playing up*.   6 Yes, I think you should *play along with him*.   7 Yes, she *passed it on*.   8 Yes, he often *plays up to him*.

62

1 putting up   2 put you up   3 put you out
4 put it off   5 put up with

63

1 be used up   2 print, duplicate   3 take control of you   4 read quickly   5 encountered

64

1 Yes, I'll *see you off*.   2 Yes, we *saw it through*.
3 Yes, I'll *see you out*.   4 Yes, we're going to *see it through*.   5 Yes, we've had it *seen to*.

65

1 in   2 off   3 up   4 back   5 on

66

1 stand in for   2 stands out   3 sat up
4 stand down   5 sat back

67

1 taking off   2 taken in   3 taking on
4 take after   5 took up with

68

1 turn up   2 turn out   3 turn him over
4 turned down   5 turn them away

69

1 He's having a *lie-in*.   2 The car's a complete *write-off*.   3 She's having a good *work-out*.
4 He's giving him a *tip-off*.   5 There's been a sudden *fall-off* in profits.   6 He's had a *breakdown*.
7 There's been a *cut-back* in expenditure.
8 He's having a *check-up*.   9 One photograph is a *blow-up* of the other.   10 There are a lot of people at the *check-out*.

70

1 mistake   2 review   3 delay   4 decrease
5 leaflet

71

1 break the ice   2 break the bank   3 break fresh ground   4 bring her to book   5 brings home the bacon   6 brought to light   7 break even
8 brought home to him

72

1 come in handy   2 came down to earth
3 came unstuck   4 come to grips with   5 come off second best

73

1 act as host   2 was the correct solution to the problem   3 producing excellent results   4 played a mean trick   5 tried as hard as possible

74

1 get a move on   2 get down to brass tacks
3 get me wrong   4 get in on the ground floor
5 got the message   6 getting nowhere
7 getting there   8 got the wind up   9 get my own back   10 got the picture clear

75

1 escape from them   2 revealed our secret
3 gave me a painful time   4 makes me feel afraid
5 provided him with a strong challenge

76

1 go spare 2 go the whole hog 3 went phut
4 going downhill 5 went by the board

77

1 have got first refusal 2 have a say 3 haven't got
a clue 4 have your wits about you 5 has got a
nerve

78

1 keep in touch 2 keep me posted 3 keep up
appearances 4 keeps himself to himself 5 kept a
tight rein on him

79

1 making his presence felt 2 made a name for
himself 3 make a dash for it 4 making light
5 make do

80

1 be second in importance 2 acts cleverly
3 involving herself in a risky situation 4 does their
share of the work 5 using his influence and good
connections 6 make a greater effort

81

1 The policeman has *caught him in the act.*/The
burglar's been *caught in the act.* 2 He's *burning the
midnight oil.* 3 He's going to *pip him at the post.*
4 He's *letting himself go.* 5 They're *waiting their
turn.* 6 She's *lost the thread* of the story. 7 Her
mother's *laying down the law.* 8 They're *comparing
notes.* 9 They are *looking daggers* at each other.
10 She's *sent him packing.*

82

1 putting the screws on us 2 put the tin lid on
3 put the firm on the map 4 put your thinking cap
on 5 put the record straight

83

1 see the sights 2 see reason 3 seen life
4 stands a fair chance 5 stand her ground
6 stand on ceremony

84

1 take sides 2 taking down a peg 3 take a dim
view of it 4 take a rise out of 5 take your pick
6 was taken for a ride 7 take it lying down
8 takes the biscuit 9 take a hint 10 took the wind
out of his sails

85

1 to throw his weight around 2 threw her off her
balance 3 throw in the towel 4 turned the corner
5 turn over a new leaf 6 turned up trumps

86

1 stick at nothing 2 Is she new to the game?
3 calling the shots 4 picked holes in
5 blowing her own trumpet 6 is asking for trouble
7 knows his onions 8 crosses swords 9 fly off the
handle 10 tell her where to get off

87

1 hold water 2 clear the air 3 call his bluff
4 picking a quarrel 5 rings a bell 6 let me off the
hook 7 lose his touch 8 bitten off more than she
can chew 9 met his match 10 rise to the occasion

88

1 open an account 2 a current account
3 draw money out 4 a deposit account
5 make out a cheque 6 a crossed cheque/an open
cheque 7 an open cheque/a crossed cheque
8 a joint account 9 bounce 10 pay in

89

1 amount 2 the drawer 3 by 4 a future date
5 you have no money in the account 6 can be
cashed by anyone who has it

90

1 makes neither profit nor loss 2 cannot pay its
debts 3 a meeting of a company's directors
4 provides a percentage of a company's capital but
takes no part in its management
5 dishonest business dealings 6 close a deal
unfairly

91

1 shop around   2 shop with   3 take goods on approval   4 on HP   5 puts prices up
6 brings prices/them down   7 knocked money off   8 selling like hot cakes   9 out of stock   10 does a roaring trade

92

1 passed away   2 on top of the world   3 worn out   4 caught a cold   5 throw it off   6 come down with   7 running a temperature   8 laid up   9 up to the mark   10 on the mend

93

1 had a smash   2 a write-off   3 The rush-hour   4 been stuck in a traffic jam   5 pulled in
6 backing out   7 jammed on the brakes   8 ran into

94

1 stands for office, runs for office   2 by new MPs   3 members of parliament who hold ministerial office   4 calls a general election   5 of the opposition party

95

1 share prices are rising   2 share prices are falling   3 industrial shares considered to be a safe investment   4 shares issued by the government   5 their nominal value, i.e. their original price

96

1 get through   2 out of order   3 gone dead   4 the line was engaged   5 a crossed line   6 put me through   7 hold the line   8 take the call   9 were cut off   10 ring off

97

1 on, By, by   2 on, take   3 off, over   4 up, made   5 in, in   6 doing

98

1 a lock-out   2 manual workers on the production line   3 a strike breaker, a blackleg, a scab   4 knock off, clock off   5 is out of work temporarily   6 do overtime   7 on the dole   8 turned down

99

1 has a bee in his bonnet   2 let the cat out of the bag   3 go to the dogs   4 cooked his goose   5 doesn't stand a cat in hell's chance   6 have butterflies in my stomach   7 Barking dogs seldom bite   8 Hold your horses   9 take the bull by the horns   10 smelt a rat

100

1 raining cats and dogs   2 cat nap   3 crocodile tears   4 up with the lark   5 making a beast   6 at a snail's pace

101

1 blue   2 red   3 black   4 green   5 blue

102

1 red herrings   2 a bolt from the blue   3 green fingers   4 black sheep   5 in his black books

103

1 himself   2 immediate subordinate   3 a person no longer regarded as important   4 he will be severely punished   5 get lucky

104

1 one in the eye for   2 one by one   3 one too many   4 one of these days   5 was one up on   6 one or two

105

1 on all fours   2 knocked him for six   3 is in two minds   4 Three cheers   5 nineteen to the dozen   6 dressed up to the nines   7 two's company   8 two heads are better than one   9 on cloud nine   10 at sixes and sevens

106

1 showed her to be less important than she leads people to believe   2 trying it to see if it pleases me   3 very close to   4 throughly   5 yield/give way at all   6 thinking about something else   7 see his disappointment very clearly   8 chatters continuously

107

1 behind her back   2 keep him at arm's length
3 give my right arm   4 see the back of it   5 be in
her blood   6 make no bones about it   7 put our
backs into it   8 have got a bone to pick with you
9 gets my blood up   10 with open arms

108

1 wet behind the ears   2 elbow grease   3 up to my
ears   4 play it by ear   5 get it off my chest
6 racking my brains

109

1 up to the eyes   2 crying her eyes out   3 see eye
to eye   4 catch his eye   5 keeping his eye peeled
6 turning a blind eye to

110

1 putting a brave face on it   2 let's face it   3 It's
staring you in the face   4 face the music   5 keep
your fingers crossed   6 has got a finger in every pie
7 all fingers and thumbs   8 put my finger on it

111

1 put his foot down   2 put my foot in it   3 put your
best foot foward   4 got off on the wrong foot
5 get back on her feet   6 didn't turn a hair
7 Keep your hair on!   8 let our hair down

112

1 keep his hand in   2 off hand   3 at first hand
4 has her hands full   5 give me a hand
6 hand over fist

113

1 is convinced   2 too difficult for me to understand
3 been good at mathematics   4 understand
5 talk for a long time   6 talking nonsense

114

1 his heart isn't in it   2 by heart   3 lose heart
4 taken it to heart   5 took to their heels   6 is on its
last legs

115

1 get it in the neck   2 broke his neck   3 is up to
the neck   4 were neck and neck   5 breathing down
my neck

116

1 paid through the nose   2 leading them by the
nose   3 keep your nose to the grindstone
4 put your shoulder to the wheel   5 giving me the
cold shoulder   6 rub shoulders with

117

1 by the skin of his teeth   2 drenched to the skin
3 gets under my skin   4 be on your toes   5 toe the
line   6 trod on her toes

118

1 hold one's tongue   2 haven't got a sweet tooth
3 bitten my tongue off   4 cut his teeth on
5 fight tooth and nail   6 got my teeth into it

119

1 call it a day   2 to the day   3 made her day
4 making a day of it   5 day by day

120

1 a night owl   2 had a night out   3 had a minute to
call my own   4 a night on the town
5 keep regular hours   6 the small hours
7 an unearthly hour   8 have my moments
9 on the spur of the moment   10 at any moment

121

1 take your time   2 time and again
3 pressed for time   4 for the time being
5 time flies   6 in time   7 doing time   8 in the
nick of time   9 in no time   10 biding her time

122

1 as cold as ice   2 as deaf as a post   3 as pleased as
Punch   4 as fit as a fiddle   5 as black as coal
6 as clear as mud

123

1 as fresh as a daisy   2 as warm as toast
3 as white as a sheet   4 as tough as leather
5 as quick as lightening   6 as old as the hills

124

1 run like a hare   2 smokes like a chimney
3 spends money like water   4 sings like a lark
5 sleeping like a log   6 looking like a drowned rat

125

1 drinks like a fish   2 shaking like a leaf   3 eats
like a horse   4 treat their employees like dirt
5 spread like wildfire   6 grinning like a Cheshire
cat